TRANSIT TRUTHS

by

GERHARD M. DAHL

TRANSIT TRUTHS

TRANSIT TRUTHS
By GERHARD M. DAHL

ERA PUBLICATIONS
New York City
1924

Transportation
Library

CONTENTS

			Page
Preface			9
Biography of Mr. Dahl			15
Chapter	I.	Organization of the B. M. T.	19
Chapter	II.	Car Rider, Taxpayer and Investor	26
Chapter	III.	Short Cut to Better Metropolitan Transit	38
Chapter	IV.	Transit Fares in Other Cities	46
Chapter	V.	Challenge to Debate	52
Chapter	VI.	Build More Transit Lines	57
Chapter	VII.	Employees Stock Ownership	73
Chapter	VIII.	Buses	76
Chapter	IX.	Shops and Yards	86
Chapter	X.	Common Sense Transit	100
Chapter	XI.	Municipal Ownership	109
Chapter	XII.	Public Officials	115
Index			119

Truth is mightier than abuse!

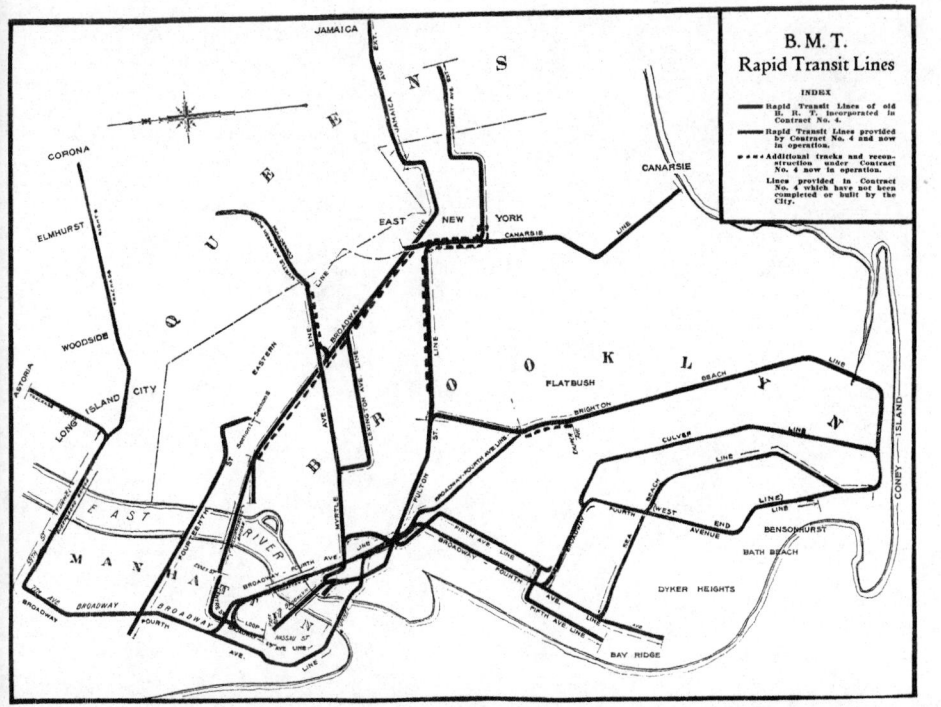

Preface

ELIMINATE politics from transit and the people of Greater New York can obtain the best transit service in the world. They may have universal service on a single fare and a comprehensive building program can be devised to provide this progressive, growing community with adequate service in the future. Everything is possible if and when *common sense* is substituted for politics in dealing with our transit problems.

Before any progress can be made, however, the public must understand the facts. After years of experience both as a public official and as a director of utility companies I have observed that when the people have the facts, and understand them, they decide soundly.

The people of New York want better transit service. Everybody acknowledges this, but, when those who are in a position to provide the money needed to give better service make constructive proposals they are abused by public officials and persecuted for daring to state facts.

From the organization of the Brooklyn-Manhattan Transit Corporation, June 15, 1923, with the support of the public directors and the other business men on the Board, we adopted the policy of taking the public into the confidence of the Company. We met representatives of the press, of civic and taxpayers' associations as well as citizens who came to the office with minor complaints about crowding and service. We listened to their statements and studied their needs. We met many public officials and political leaders. But everywhere, we found that there were very few citizens who understood or who knew the primary facts about transit.

This convinced me that my first duty as Chairman of the Board was to contribute all the facts I knew or could obtain to the general public discussion of transit. During the past year I have written a number of important letters to the Mayor of New York City; to the Transit Commission of New York State and to the Chairman of the Board of Transportation of New York City. Many statements have been issued to the press on all phases of transit. On two occasions page advertisements were published in all the leading daily and weekly newspapers in the city. Several public speeches were made before civic bodies. All of this was done for the sole purpose of giving information to the people of this city on the most critical problem confronting them.

Although many of the most important statements have been printed in booklet form they are gathered together in this volume for the convenience of those who want *facts*.

"History has brought into partnership the transit companies and the City in the great subway system of the community," said the Brooklyn *Times*, December 19, 1923. "In the past the partners have been warring members of the owning firm. While they battled the public service suffered."

Because this condition existed, the B. M. T., from the very beginning of its work, decided upon a policy of full and frank co-operation with the City and the public. In pursuit of this policy, its record is:

   1. Reorganized 592 miles (single track) of subway, elevated and surface lines in Brooklyn, Queens and Manhattan on a sound financial basis.

Preface

2. Elected directors to represent the public.

3. Paid $2,200,000 in personal injury claims against old B. R. T.

4. Purchased 50 new steel subway cars.

5. Spent $4,000,000 on new equipment and improvements.

6. Designed and built duplex trolley car.

7. Offered to operate the Ashland Place Connection at an estimated ultimate minimum cost to the Company of $5,000,000 for construction and equipment.

8. Opened and operated Western Half of new 14th Street-Eastern Line.

9. Purchased 10 modern buses and offered to operate bus routes in Brooklyn and Queens at cost and to operate buses experimentally on 3 routes for a period of 3 months at a 5 cent fare with free transfers to intersecting rapid transit and surface lines of the B. M. T. System.

10. Consented to the modification of Contract No. 4 to permit the construction of the 14th Street-Eastern Line as a subway to East New York, thus ending 5 years deadlock over the construction of this line.

11. Requested City to live up to Contract 4, signed March 19, 1913 and complete Nassau link in lower Manhattan, 14th Street Line to East New York and build shops and yards.

12. Spent $530,000 on new "oil" switches and other safety improvements in the Williamsburg Power Plant.

Transit Truths

13. Offered to finance the construction and equipment of all subway lines needed by the City.

14. Offered to provide full steel equipment on all its rapid transit lines if and when the City built a new tunnel under the East River so that wooden cars could be removed from lines operating over Brooklyn Bridge.

15. Offered to revise Contract 4 and meet the City officials in conference to devise ways and means of providing full and complete transit lines and service for the public.

16. Conducted a referendum among the passengers on the Brighton and Utica Avenue lines to determine the desires of the car riders in regard to proposed changes in service.

17. Opened the new Lawrence Street station in the heart of Brooklyn's downtown business center.

Almost from the very beginning, however, the B. M. T. has met with the bitter, personal and unfair opposition of Mayor Hylan with the result that there is no other alternative for the Company than that of continuing its dual program of giving the best service possible with existing facilities subject to political manipulation and at the same time giving full information to the public. The people themselves will settle the transit problem when they understand the facts.

During 1923, nearly $300,000,000 was spent on new building construction in Brooklyn alone. During this same period practically nothing was appropriated by the City of New York for additional transit facilities.

Preface

This record of inaction is only comparable to the eleven years' delay by the City in completing the contract signed March 19, 1913.

The issue before the people resolves itself finally into this:

Shall transit be treated as a business problem? Shall subways be built? Shall the people have service? Or—shall cheap politics continue to block subway construction and force added discomforts and congestion?

From the beginning the B. M. T. has been willing to meet all the public needs on a fair, business basis. Confident that this program will be endorsed by the car riders, taxpayers and investors because it is the only program which can guarantee adequate service, I am willing to continue the policy we have followed for the past year.

GERHARD M. DAHL.

New York City,
October, 1924.

Biography of Mr. Dahl

By Carl W. Ackerman

MR. DAHL'S report of today is truly a report of progress."

This sentence from an editorial in the Brooklyn *Standard Union* strikes the keynote of Gerhard Melvin Dahl's activities in behalf of Better Metropolitan Transit in Greater New York. After 14 years' experience directing the affairs of transit companies and other public utilities in Cleveland, New Orleans and other cities, Mr. Dahl assumed a large share of responsibility in the organization of the Brooklyn-Manhattan Transit Corporation. Since March, 1923, first as a member of the Reorganization Committee and then as Chairman of the Board of Directors, the policies which he formulated and championed have laid the foundation for public understanding and discussion of New York City's transit problems because they have been *progressive*.

There are two fundamental principles back of Chairman Dahl's policies. The first is that the public right to service and the Company's rights as a business institution, are equally entitled to a "square deal." The second is that the Company's dual obligation is to provide service and state facts. Throughout the correspondence and letters published in this book these two themes are emphasized, —service and information.

Mr. Dahl has absolute confidence in public judgment based upon facts. This faith in public opinion is an outgrowth of his experience as a public official in Wisconsin and Ohio and as a director in utilities serving the public in all parts of the United States. He has observed public actions both as an office holder and as a business man. The guiding principle behind his own actions in public life, in the practice of law and in business has been one of absolute frankness.

Gerhard Melvin Dahl is what Bruce Barton defined as a New York man when he wrote, during the War, "I am New York." The people of New York, he said, "make their way to me from North and South, from the East and from the West . . . as the home of opportunity. . . . They are the builders who have made me (New York City) great, and on what foundation stones, think you, have they built? On money? On commerce? On trade? They have wrought with materials more eternal. They have laid my foundations on FAITH."

Mr. Dahl brought this faith with him to New York from Wisconsin and Ohio. Born of sturdy Norwegian stock in Ft. Howard, Wisconsin, June 8, 1876, he studied law and graduated from the University of Wisconsin. While practicing law he was elected to public office, first as City Attorney of Waupaca and then as district attorney of Portage County, Wisconsin. His record in Wisconsin won recognition not only at home but in Ohio and on November 1, 1906, after nearly four years as a public official he resigned to accept a position with one of the largest and most important law firms in Cleveland, Ohio, M. B. and H. H. Johnson. He remained with this firm until he was appointed Street Railroad Commissioner of Cleveland in which office he served a term of two years.

Thus for six years, as a public official, he had ample opportunity to study public opinion which led him to the conclusion that the right kind of public policy, when made known to the public would win out against ignorance and abuse.

Mr. Dahl's first intimate knowledge of transit problems was gained in Cleveland.

After ten years of bitter political controversy over renewal of franchises and rates of fare in Cleveland, Ohio, the street railway problem was settled the latter part of February, 1910, at a referendum of all the voters of Cleveland by the adoption of a cost of service plan under which the value of the property of the Cleveland Railway Company and the rate of return which it was entitled to earn on that value were agreed to. This agreement was ratified at the polls by a large majority of the voters of Cleveland.

This cost of service plan went into effect on March 1, 1910. That plan provided for a Street Railroad Commissioner to be appointed by the city, to see that its interests were thoroughly protected. Mr. Dahl was appointed the first Street Railroad Commissioner under that plan by Mayor Herman C. Baehr and took office on March 1, 1910. At that time the rate of fare was three cents with one cent for a transfer. On June 1, 1911, Mr. Dahl reduced the fare by cutting out the charge for transfer and the rate of fare was therefore three cents with free transfers which continued until September 1, 1914.

Mr. Dahl occupied this position until January 1, 1912. On June 1, 1912, he came to New York and became Vice President of the Electric Bond and Share Company which is engaged in financing and managing public utilities in many states in the Union. The Electric Bond and Share Company is one of the largest public utility bankers and managers in the United States. Its properties are operated with conspicuous success and with a thorough regard for the welfare of the public.

On January 1, 1917, Mr. Dahl became Vice President of The Chase National Bank. While occupying this position, he was called upon to reorganize the New Orleans Railway and Light Company. Three years were required to complete this task and the company was successfully reorganized in the fall of 1922 and has since been operating successfully and with the approval of the public of New Orleans.

Supported by a strong board of directors representing both the public and the 26,000 investors in the B. M. T., Chairman Dahl has been assisted by President William S. Menden's thirteen years' practical experience with the operation of transit lines in Chicago and nineteen years in Greater New York, by Vice President Travis H. Whitney's intimate knowledge of transit needs following his experience first as Secretary and later as a member of the Public Service Commission and by George D. Yeoman's services as Vice President and General Counsel.

The reader will observe in the following chapters that Mr. Dahl's leadership has been an active leadership and that in endeavoring to obtain ACTION by the City he has contributed to the progress of public thought innumerable sound proposals which will lead ultimately to a practical and serviceable solution of New York City's tangled transit problems.

TRANSIT TRUTHS

Chapter I.
Organization of the B. M. T.

IN 1913 when the public requirements for new rapid transit facilities were beyond the capacity of city capital, the City of New York entered into dual contracts with the existing operating companies. They were the Interborough Rapid Transit Company and the Brooklyn Rapid Transit Company. Under these contracts the City agreed to finance and build certain new lines and the companies obligated themselves to contribute money towards cost of construction of City lines. to reconstruct and extend their own lines and to equip and operate all lines as unified systems on a five cent fare for a period of 49 years. These contracts were known as the "Dual Subway Contracts."

Under these contracts the City of New York and the private companies became partners in the business of rapid transit. On December 31, 1918, the B. R. T. was forced into the hands of a receiver appointed by the federal courts. A reorganization committee was formed to examine the position of the B. R. T., and formulate a plan of reorganizing the company on a firm financial foundation.

On March 15, 1923, a plan of reorganization was perfected and at great financial sacrifices the owners of the B. R. T. securities were asked to join in the formation of the Brooklyn-Manhattan Transit Corporation. The result of the receivership, the failure of the City to live up to its contract, the tremendous increase in operating expenses and the cost of money was that every private investor who, in 1912 invested $1,000 in the bonds of the B. R. T. System, lost $433. This was the fate of thousands of investors who owned the securities of the old company. Stockholders, on the other hand, lost practically everything and paid an assessment of $35 per share, amounting to $26,000,000, which additional sum has been devoted to giving the people service. I recall the letter of a school teacher who wrote me recently that she had had $2,000 invested in B. R. T. securities and when she finally received her new stock in the reorganization and received a return on the preferred stock of the B. M. T., she cried for joy. She is not the only person who has held on to the stock. She is not the only one whose losses in B. R. T. have by no means been made up by the normal appreciation in the securities of the B. M. T. There are many others who owned B. R. T. common stock when it sold as high as $138 a share on the New York Stock Exchange and who saw their savings dwindle to nothing. Many of these stockholders are still among the 26,000 owners of B. M. T. common and preferred stock. Among our stockholders are over 10,000 employees.

In assuming the direction of one of the great transportation systems of this city the new directors were faced by terrific problems of costs and service. The elevated, subway and surface lines of the Company extended like a gridiron over the congested and residential sections of three boroughs, Brooklyn, Queens and Manhattan. Three thousand cars were to be operated each day to transport 2,250,000 passengers.

The costs of material and wages were over 100 per

Organization of the B. M. T.

cent higher in 1923 when the B. M. T. was organized than they were in 1913. In the Way and Structure Department (surface lines) men who received 20 cents an hour in 1913 were receiving 47 cents per hour. Motormen on rapid transit lines had their wages increased from $35\frac{1}{2}$ cents per hour in 1913 to 78 cents per hour in 1923. Wages in the power plant jumped from 28 cents per hour to 65 cents in 1923.

Modern steel subway cars which cost $15,000 each fully equipped in 1913, cost $35,000 in 1923. Brake shoes which cost $30 per ton in 1913 advanced to $70 per ton ten years later. Rails for surface lines which were $39 per gross ton in 1913 were costing $48 when the B. M. T. began business.

Assuming that during the year 1923, the rates of pay for labor and the prices for materials as existed in 1913 were applied, the total labor and material charge would have been $13,800,000. Instead of this the total labor and material costs for the year ending March 31, 1923, were $28,000,000, an increase of $14,200,000.

To cope with these problems of costs, the big financial problems involved, the public needs and demands for more adequate transit, and the hostile attitude of city officials toward all aspects of transit, a strong, representative and working body of directors was needed.

Before the Board was formed we made special inquiry in Brooklyn, Queens and Manhattan and asked for suggestions as to the most public spirited and unselfish business men, who had no interest in transit securities, who could and would represent the public. Many excellent recommendations were made and the selection was difficult although, in the end, men of high public standing and unassailable reputation joined with other business men in the creation of a new Board of Directors, represent-

Transit Truths

ing the public, the Transit Commission, the United States Government and the stockholders and bondholders.

Since June 15, 1923, these men, with one exception, are still serving on the Board of Directors, which is proof that the affairs of the Company have met with their unqualified support. The exception, however, is due not to the policy of the Company but to the fact that Mr. Travis H. Whitney, former Public Service Commissioner, resigned from the Board to devote his entire time to the affairs of the system as Vice President.

The directors of the company today are:

ARTHUR S. SOMERS
President, Brooklyn Chamber of Commerce, Brooklyn

CHARLES A. BOODY
President, Peoples Trust Co., Brooklyn

J. SHERLOCK DAVIS
President, Cross, Austin & Ireland, and former President of Brooklyn Chamber of Commerce, Brooklyn

JAMES H. POST
President, National Sugar Refining Co., Brooklyn

WILLIAM H. JOHNS
President, George Batten Company, and former President of Queensboro Chamber of Commerce, Queens

WILLIAM H. ENGLISH
Director, Brooklyn Trust Co., Brooklyn

ROBERT ALFRED SHAW
Member, Transit Committee of the Brooklyn Chamber of Commerce, Brooklyn

ALFRED E. MARLING
Former President, Chamber of Commerce, New York, Manhattan

WILLIAM S. MENDEN
President, Brooklyn-Manhattan Transit Corp., Brooklyn

GEORGE S. FRANKLIN
Cotton and Franklin, Manhattan

Organization of the B. M. T.

ALBERT H. WIGGIN
President, The Chase National Bank, Manhattan

FREDERICK STRAUSS
J. & W. Seligman & Co., Manhattan

MATTHEW C. BRUSH
President, American International Corp., Manhattan

CHARLES S. SARGENT, JR.
Kidder, Peabody & Company, Manhattan

GERHARD M. DAHL
Hayden, Stone & Company, Manhattan

In terminating the receivership of the B. R. T., in the United States District Court, Judge Julius M. Mayer said:

"The new Board consists of residents of the three boroughs through which these rapid transit properties are operated. Well-known men of substantial affairs necessarily interested in the welfare of the city at large have been selected as directors.

"The new Board thus consists of real directors and not of dummies or of men unknown in the community. These men bring to the new Board the character and equipment which are vital to the success of such a great transportation system. I am confident that it is their purpose so to conduct the affairs of this system as to serve the public and invite its confidence while at the same time exercising that care and supervision to which the investors, who have put many millions of dollars in these properties, are fully entitled."

Addressing the members of the Brooklyn Chamber of Commerce, within a few months after his election to the B. M. T. Board, Mr. Arthur S. Somers, who is now serving his second term as President of that organization, interpreted the letters, "B. M. T." to mean "Better Metropolitan Transit."

In the course of his address, President Somers said:

"When the financial reorganization committee determined to pay the victims of the unfortunate Malbone Street disaster $2,200,000 they were not only actuated by a desire to adjust a debt but they were determined to start with a clean slate.

"Safety First with this company is a policy and not a slogan.

"Again when the directors appropriated nearly two million dollars for 50 new subway cars; again when the management, under the able direction of Mr. William S. Menden, who has for 19 years grown with the transit system of Brooklyn, conducted the Brighton Ballot to determine the preference of the passengers in regard to service, the B. M. T. showed by its actions that it was inspired by a desire to give service, the best service possible under the handicaps of existing costs and conditions.

"But," Mr. Somers concluded, "as the B. M. T. newspaper says, let us 'Look Ahead.' Our prosperity, our happiness, our success, our comforts depend upon the New York of tomorrow, the New York of bigger, better, cleaner transit facilities, because I believe the public is willing to co-operate with the Company and that the Company and the public are willing to co-operate with the City in solving our transit problems.

"So, I commend to you, to the people of Brooklyn, Queens and Manhattan, that we make this policy our policy because it is one upon which we can all unite. There is nothing the directors and management of the B. M. T. system seek, there is nothing the public desires,

Organization of the B. M. T.

there is nothing the city administration can ask for, which can exceed the possibilities of the policy which the letters B. M. T. should stand for, namely,

"Better Metropolitan Transit."

This policy was adopted and pursued by the Company. It is still the policy of the Company although, as the following letters and statements show, the Company has had no co-operation whatsoever from the City.

Chapter II.
Car Rider, Taxpayer and Investor

ON January 23, 1924, I spoke at the first public meeting of the Civic Council of Brooklyn and the annual dinner of the Queensboro Chamber of Commerce.

On those occasions I said:

"Everybody in this city today is demanding better rapid transit service and new subway lines. Each day there is a new appeal. Not only from the crowded subway trains but from the business men and residents of Queens, Brooklyn and Manhattan. We all agree that conditions are disgraceful and dangerous. There is no question but what subway construction has been too long delayed. Building of additional subways should have commenced long ago. Immediate relief is impossible, for even though construction were begun today it will take several years before the additional subways will be available for use. It is vital, therefore, that action should take the place of discussion. But the subway problem in this community will never be solved until the public faces the cold, hard facts which are financial and not political.

"Harmony between public officials having charge of subway construction is of importance, but the real problem is a lack of understanding of the facts by the public of this great community, and until they do understand the facts, there can be no real solution of the transit problem. There are men in this community who understand the facts and whose duty it is to present these facts to

Car Rider, Taxpayer and Investor

the public, but the real facts are such that no public official, no one who aspires to hold public office, no one who is ambitious for popularity has had the courage to present them.

"In order to make the facts simple and understandable, I have divided the community into three classes of people: The Car Rider, the Taxpayer, the Investor.

"The car rider wants rapid and convenient service whenever he needs to go from one place to another. He is not interested in the economics of transportation. He does not concern himself with the costs of service. He does not care whether it costs five or fifty cents to carry him so long as he does not have to pay more than a nickel. He considers that the community or the company has an obligation to transport him with that maximum of comfort and convenience and that minimum of expense which he considers ideal. He is very apt to complain and resent any infringement upon the standard which he has set up. But the car rider today should receive sympathy and not criticism.

"The car rider may or may not be an investor or a taxpayer, and so long as he does not come within the last two classes he comes within the description which I have given. He pays five cents for a ride.

The Taxpayer

"The taxpayer falls within the second group. This is the group which is the backbone of the city. The taxpayers provide the money for our city, state and national governments. They provided large sums of money for subways. The taxpayer may or may not be an investor, he may or may not be a car rider. As he must pay taxes, either directly to the city or indirectly in rent or the cost of living, he is interested in paying only those taxes which in justice and fairness he should pay. The taxpayer, if he rides in the subways, pays five cents directly but an additional fare indirectly by his taxes because the money he has invested, through the city in subways, has not earned interest.

"The investor may belong to either of the preceding groups, or he may not. He may be an individual or a life insurance company or a savings bank. The company which insures you or the bank where you keep your money may be an investor. The investor is interested primarily in the security of his investment. He has placed a certain sum of money at the disposal of the company and he expects that the company will administer its affairs so that he will get a return on that investment. He expects the community to treat the company fairly so that the company will be enabled to earn a return on that investment.

"Investors who use our subways must pay the regular five cent fare plus the extra amount paid by the taxpayer and plus the amount of interest and principal which they have lost during the past ten years in New York rapid transit stocks and bonds.

FUTURE INVESTORS

"Investors might also be divided into present and future investors. The present investor has his money already in and he can only get out by selling at a sacrifice. Every man and woman, every insurance company or savings bank having invested in securities of transportation companies in Greater New York since the dual contracts were made in 1913 have lost money.

"The future investor, however, is in a different cate-

Car Rider, Taxpayer and Investor

gory. Before he puts any money into rapid transit lines he is going to be sure that the business he invests in is going to make money and not lose it. Therefore, we cannot build or equip new subway lines in this city in the future unless the future investor has confidence in the transit business—in transit as a business proposition. That is, private investors will not put any more money into transit equipment unless their investment is secure and interest on the investment is to be earned.

WHAT HAS HAPPENED?

"As there are only two groups of citizens who can finance new subway lines or their equipment, what has been their experience in this city? It is evident to everyone that either the taxpayer or the investor must bear the burden, jointly or severally.

"What has happened to these three, the Car Rider, the Taxpayer and the Investor, during the past ten years?

"The car rider is suffering daily. I do not have to describe his condition because you are all familiar with it. I only need to point out that during the past ten years no adequate measures have been taken for his relief.

"The taxpayer, during the last ten years, has contributed to the cost of transporting the car rider. The City has invested in our rapid transit lines $150,000,000 and in the lines of the Interborough $100,000,000 on which it is not getting one cent of return. The taxpayer is paying the interest on $250,000,000 of bonds issued to produce the cash used for building subways.

"The investor has lost money in the last ten years. I am not speaking now about stockholders but about bondholders—those who invested their money in bonds of transit companies expecting to get a modest return and who thought they had adequate security.

"Ten years ago a subsidiary of the old B. R. T. made a contract with the City which is known as Contract No. 4. It will soon be eleven years old. By the terms of this contract it was agreed that the Company—or, in other words, the investor—should have 6% on its investment before the City got any return on the taxpayer's money. The agreed return which the Company was to have was described as preferentials. The existing rapid transit lines in Brooklyn at that time were considered as having an earning capacity of $3,500,000 and it was agreed that the Company should have $3,500,000 plus 6% on the new money before the City received any return.

"In considering the Company's investment, therefore, I have capitalized that $3,500,000 at 6% and, when I hereafter speak of the Company's investment, it is understood that I refer to 6% on the new money and the $3,500,000 capitalized at 6%.

INCREASED COSTS

"By the terms of the contract the City agreed to build certain subways and the Company—or the investor—agreed to equip and operate the lines for a five cent fare. At that time it was estimated that the total cost to the City would be $104,500,000—I am dealing now only with the lines of the old B. R. T. Company. It was estimated that the cost to the Company would be $60,000,000. The cost to the City to date has been nearly $150,000,000 and the cost to the Company $86,000,000 and the work covered by the original contract is not yet finished. In other words, instead of earning interest and sinking fund on a total of

Car Rider, Taxpayer and Investor

$164,500,000 as was originally estimated, it became necessary with the same facilities and with the same five cent fare to earn interest and sinking fund on $236,000,000.

"Now, I am told by those who are more familiar with the history of transit in this community than I am that the increased cost was due to delay on the part of the public authorities and that if the taxpayer had proceeded with business-like expedition in carrying out his contract it would not have been necessary for the investor to raise as much money to carry out his part of the contract. Of course the authorities insist that the war was responsible for the delay and something may be said to support that contention. And still the Eastern section of the 14th Street Line and the Nassau-Broad Street Line are not completed.

"Now, instead of earning 6% on its investment during the past ten years, the Company has earned varying percentages constituting an average for ten years of 3.83%.

"If instead of paying a five cent fare, the car rider had paid 5.79 cents it would have produced 6% on the Company's investment, but still nothing on the City's investment. If you add the City's investment to the Company's investment and then figure the actual earnings for the past ten years, you find that a five cent fare produced 1.96% on the total investment.

A Ride Cost 7.31 Cents

"During all of this time, the car rider paid five cents. If he had paid 7.31 cents it would have produced 6% on the Company's investment and actual interest on the City's investment. The car rider, therefore, in the past ten years, has been getting a ride for five cents which cost 7.31 cents. The other 2.31 cents has been paid by the taxpayer and the investor. If a merchant bought calico at 7.31 cents a yard and sold it at 5 cents a yard, how long would he last? If he got to the end of his resources and the taxpayer stepped in to help him, how long would the taxpayer continue to carry that burden?

"Now, I am not asking for a higher rate of fare. I am not initiating any propaganda against a five cent fare. Bear that in mind. But I want you to understand the facts so that you will know that when you want more service which costs more money—and practically all additional service costs more money—that the car rider is getting for five cents what costs 7.31 cents, and that while the investor recognizes the fact that the car rider needs more and better service and is willing and anxious to give it to him, that he has suffered about all the loss he can and that he cannot give 7½ cent or 8 cent service for five cents. If the taxpayer is willing to contribute the extra amount required, then the investor, of course, should not complain. He should welcome it because the investor recognizes the necessity for additional service.

ACCUMULATED DEFICITS

"Now, what is the situation of the taxpayer today?

"By the terms of Contract 4, if the investor failed to get his annual interest, it became cumulative. In other words, it was agreed that the investor should have 6% from the beginning and the City should have no return until that had occurred. These are what is known as preferentials. As a result, the investor is $14,500,000 behind the game. These are the accumulated deficits during the past ten years. And before the taxpayer can receive any return, the investor must receive his current 6% and the accumulated preferentials of $14,500,000. And what is the position of the taxpayer as to the question of extensions? The Company is obliged by the terms of the contract to spend money for equipping and to operate the extensions. For instance, the Brooklyn Crosstown Line may be located wherever the public authorities decide. We have nothing to say about it. And the public can operate it separately if they want to and we cannot complain. But, if the City elects, we are obliged to spend millions of dollars to equip and operate it, provided that, if it loses money, the taxpayer pays the deficit. In other words, if it costs seven cents to carry passengers on any extension and the car rider pays five cents, the taxpayer must pay the other two cents. The investor cannot be compelled to contribute to any loss except such as may arise from the operation of the subways described in the original contract.

$165,000,000 NEEDED

"What is the capacity of the taxpayer to finance additional subway construction? According to the report of the Comptroller the total unreserved margin within the debt limit as of August 3, 1923, was $76,000,000. The additional lines, under construction, or proposed, are estimated to cost $165,000,000. The Brooklyn Crosstown Line as a four-track subway, is estimated to cost $68,700,000; the Washington Heights subway is estimated to cost $67,500,000; the Nassau Street Branch, $13,500,000; the 14th Street-Eastern as a subway, $11,000,000, and the Ashland Place Connection, $4,450,000. And if the total unreserved margin within the debt limit should be absorbed for subway construction, what about additional public improvements which are required for the welfare of the people of this community.

"Of course, when new subway lines are built, the subways greatly increase the value of property but this increase in the value of property is not in proportion to the growing needs of the city. When subways go into new sections they may add a hundred million dollars to the assessed value of property but this amount of increased borrowing power is more than eaten up by the cost of new schools, public improvements and the thousand and one administrative expenses which come along with the subway traffic. The result is that the progress of New York is rapidly overcoming its present ability to finance subways and public improvements unless subway lines in the future are placed on a business basis so that they pay both the taxpayers and the investors a fair return on their investments.

"It must be obvious to anyone that the only reason New York has maintained a five cent fare during the period of the War and since is because the taxpayer and the investor together have held the bag. In other communities throughout the United States where the taxpayer had no money invested fares were raised, not so much out of justice to the investor as out of necessity in order to attract the future investor. In practically every other city in the United States the transportation system is surface and not subway and, of course, the capital expenditure is less for a surface line than for a subway line and, therefore, the cost of carrying car riders is less including in cost a fair return on the capital invested. Therefore, the rate of fare should be higher in New York than elsewhere. But, of course, the contrary is true. In the chief cities in the country, including New York, the rate of fare in 1913 was five cents. That was true of Chicago, Philadelphia, Detroit, St. Louis, Boston, Baltimore, Buffalo and Pittsburgh. Today the rate of fare is five cents in not a single one of those cities. In Chicago it is ten cents and seven cents; in Boston ten cents; in Pittsburgh ten cents and in the other cities seven cents and six cents.

NOT ADVOCATING HIGHER FARE

"I want to repeat that from the viewpoint of the selfish interests of the B. M. T., I am not advocating a higher fare. The B. M. T. can live on a five cent fare because it is the reorganized product of the old B. R. T. Thousands of investors have taken their losses. The stockholders have come to the front and have raised and put into the new company $26,000,000 in order to protect their interests, and we believe we can work out the situation on a five cent fare so far as our own selfish interests are concerned. But, from the viewpoint of the interests of the community, I must say to you that while we can live on a five cent fare, we cannot possibly expand and develop and give the community the kind of service to which it is entitled unless the taxpayer is willing to pay the difference between five cents and what it costs to carry the car rider.

"But we do have the right to urge upon the City that it shall fufill its part of the contract. Nearly eleven years ago the City agreed to build the Nassau Street Branch and the 14th Street-Eastern Line. Today the 14th Street-Eastern Line remains uncompleted and the Nassau Street Branch has not been touched. The Nassau Street Branch is not only in the interests of the Company, but in the interests of the car rider, for its construction would tremendously improve the efficiency of the service between Brooklyn and Manhattan. The completion of the 14th Street-Eastern Line is of vital importance to the car riders because it would relieve the unbearable and almost unspeakable conditions at Canal Street. And these are lines which the City agreed to build eleven years ago. They are not new lines. Furthermore, by Contract No. 4 the City agreed to supply car shops for the Company which have not yet been built. The taxpayer has insisted that the investor should live up to the letter of his contract by charging a five cent fare while the taxpayer, on the other hand, has failed to live up to the contract so far as he was concerned by refusing to construct Nassau Street, by refusing to build the 14th Street-Eastern Line and by refusing to supply car shops, although all of these things are specifically covered by the contract.

Who Will Hold the Bag?

"To sum up the situation from the viewpoint of the welfare of the community and not from the viewpoint of any selfish or financial interest, not from the viewpoint of the investor, but from the viewpoint of the car rider and the taxpayer there are these fundamental questions:

"First, the City and the subway companies have raised and expended for building and equipping subways in the last ten years approximately $500,000,000. As much, if not more, will be needed in the next ten years. Where is the money coming from? Can the taxpayer supply it? Will he if he can?

"Second, the car riders have failed to pay the cost of carrying them in the subways in the last ten years to the extent of $84,968,800. The taxpayer and the investor together have paid this deficit. The investor cannot continue to pay a similar deficit for the next ten years. Who will hold the bag? Can the taxpayer do it? Will he if he can?"

TEN YEARS' EXPERIENCE OF THE TAXPAYER AND THE INVESTOR

Year	Average Investment	Required Earnings for Actual Interest on City Investment and 6% Return on Company Investment	Actual Earnings	Equivalent to % Per Annum	Required Fare Per Passenger for Required Earnings
1914	$111,311,681.87	$ 5,530,070.63	$2,975,759	2.67	$.065
1915	136,254,719.41	7,393,639.87	3,265,275	2.40	.075
1916	164,334,880.91	8,465,743.54	3,924,467	2.39	.073
1917	191,311,355.26	9,661,106.64	4,358,451	2.28	.074
1918	219,385,684.23	11,150,387.45	4,760,451	2.17	.075
1919	239,580,315.07	12,084,990.88	4,331,680	1.80	.075
1920	256,815,616.52	13,048,756.41	3,542,008	1.38	.075
1921	270,990,290.24	14,044,938.89	1,414,177	.52	.081
1922	282,299,595.16	14,681,821.73	6,640,557	2.36	.068
*1923	289,751,631.06	16,278,991.88	7,264,324	2.50	.069
Average for 10-Year Period	$216,203,576.97	$11,234,044.79	$4,247,715	1.96	.0731

*1923 partly estimated.

INVESTORS' TEN YEARS' EXPERIENCE WITH RAPID TRANSIT

Year	Average Investment	Required Earnings for 6% Return	Actual Earnings	Equivalent to % Per Annum	Required Fare Per Passenger for Required Earnings
1914	$ 64,104,364	$3,846,261.86	$2,975,759	4.64	$.055
1915	81,978,103	4,918,686.19	3,265,275	3.98	.060
1916	94,439,363	5,666,361.79	3,924,467	4.15	.059
1917	102,969,130	6,178,147.80	4,358,451	4.25	.058
1918	112,331,758	6,739,905.47	4,760,451	4.23	.058
1919	117,848,569	7,070,914.12	4,331,680	3.67	.059
1920	123,304,531	7,398,271.84	3,542,008	2.87	.060
1921	130,148,642	7,808,918.55	1,414,177	1.08	.066
1922	136,982,390	8,218,943.41	6,640,557	4.84	.054
*1923	142,270,833	8,536,250.00	7,264,324	5.10	.053
Average for 10-Year Period	$110,637,768	$6,638,266.10	$4,247,715	3.83	.0579

*1923 partly estimated.

Chapter III.
Short Cut to Better Metropolitan Transit

ON December 18, 1923, the following program suggesting a "short cut" to Better Metropolitan Transit was outlined to the public:

The Transit Commission and several civic organizations have asked the B. M. T. directors for a statement of policy toward the proposed "Ashland Place Connection." Other public bodies have asked us to agree to change our contract with the City so that the eastern portion of the 14th Street Line may be constructed as a subway instead of an elevated. Likewise, as a result of the dangerous increase in traffic at Canal Street we received numerous requests for information as to why the 14th Street Line and the Nassau-Broad Street Extension are not built.

These inquiries all mean that the people of this city want additional rapid transit lines and that they want to know now whether they can or cannot have them. This is as true of the Ashland Place Connection between Fulton Street "L" and the Fourth Avenue subway as it is of the 14th Street-Eastern and the Nassau Street lines.

With these needs and desires of the traveling public the directors of this company are in absolute accord.

At the November, 1923, meeting of the Board of Directors a special committee was appointed to study the proposed "Ashland Place Connection." As soon as this committee, consisting of Messrs. Robert Alfred

Shaw, Arthur S. Somers, Travis H. Whitney, William S. Menden and myself, began to study this problem we discovered that it was impossible to patch the system without giving patched service. The committee recommended, therefore, that the Ashland Place Connection, the 14th Street-Eastern and the Nassau-Broad Street Lines be considered as a unit.

DIRECTORS APPROVE PROGRAM TO INCREASE AND BETTER SERVICE

Accepting this recommendation the directors at their December meeting approved a program which if carried out will provide for at least 50 per cent additional train capacity through DeKalb Avenue, will eliminate the inconvenience and congestion at Canal Street and provide real relief in the form of additional rapid transit service for the people of East New York, Central Brooklyn, South Brooklyn and 14th Street, Manhattan.

The directors of this Company are already on record (announcement of November 21, 1923) favoring more rapid transit lines whether we operate them or not, but in three specific instances we have both a duty and an obligation. These we call to the attention of the public because the initiative now rests with the City and not with the B. M. T.

THE FOURTEENTH STREET-EASTERN LINE

1. Dual subway Contract No. 4, signed March 19, 1913, is still binding between the City of New York and the Company. Under this contract the City agreed to construct the 14th Street-Eastern Line. This has not been completed. We are ready, however, to operate this line whenever the City finishes the work. We have been

asked whether we will consent to a change in our contract so that the eastern portion may be constructed as a subway. As the public demand for this change evidently expresses the public need we will agree to this change in the contract provided our present legal rights and claims are adequately preserved and the subway is constructed under plans which will connect it with our existing structures at East New York, but we wish to point out to the public that this Company expended years ago in anticipation of the early completion of this line approximately $500,000 third-tracking the Myrtle Avenue "L," which includes an express station at Wyckoff Avenue to connect with the 14th Street-Eastern Line. This expenditure will be wasted unless facilities are provided for the convenient transfer of passengers between the 14th Street Line and the Myrtle Avenue Line at this point. Therefore it should be understood in case the contract is modified so as to provide for substitution of subway for elevated construction, that the City will provide suitable and adequate facilities for transfer of passengers between the subway and elevated lines at Myrtle and Wyckoff Avenues, in order that the third track and station facilities already provided by the Company may be utilized.

NASSAU-BROAD STREET LINE

2. The second plank in our program of action is the construction of the Nassau-Broad Street Line. This is also an unfulfilled part of Contract No. 4. The B. M. T. is ready to equip and operate this line as soon as the City constructs it. Furthermore, as a part of this contract the City agreed to build shops and yards. These are urgently needed in order to maintain even the present service. When the Nassau-Broad Street Line is built and

Short Cut to Better Metropolitan Transit

the 14th Street-Eastern Line is completed, the present 50,000 daily victims of the Canal Street blockade will receive the direct relief which they demand and need.

ASHLAND PLACE CONNECTION

3. The third plank relates to the proposed connection between the Fulton Street "L" and the Fourth Avenue system at Ashland Place. The B. M. T. is entirely willing to sign a contract for the Ashland Place Connection as soon as it has definite and tangible assurance that the City will construct and complete the 14th Street-Eastern and the Nassau Street Lines.

This program is the shortest cut to additional rapid transit service for the people of Brooklyn and lower Manhattan.

PROBLEMS INVOLVED IN CONSTRUCTION OF ASHLAND PLACE CONNECTION

As the people of Brooklyn are so vitally interested in the Ashland Place Connection we wish to state, briefly, some of the problems involved in this improvement because it is only through a mutual understanding of both sides of public questions that the public needs can be met.

CONGESTION AT DEKALB AVENUE—THE HEART OF B. M. T. IN BROOKLYN

The DeKalb Avenue station is not only the heart of the B. M. T. rapid transit system in Brooklyn, but directly affects the proposed Ashland Place Connection. Today sixteen tracks radiate south and east in Brooklyn and serve great and growing communities. These are the 2-track Fourth Avenue Line, south of Fifty-ninth Street; the 4-track Sea Beach Line; the 3-track West End

Transit Truths

Line; the 3-track Culver Line and 4 tracks of the Brighton Line. Passengers carried by these lines destined for downtown Brooklyn and Manhattan, with the possible exception of the Culver Line passengers en route to Park Row, pass through or transfer at DeKalb Avenue station. The group of tracks at this station today is inadequate for this traffic. The station has only two platforms for six tracks, two of which are through tracks having no platform facilities. Because of these limited facilities and because of the dam at Chambers Street, Manhattan, due to the lack of the Nassau-Broad Street Extension, the B. M. T. cannot operate more than 60 trains per hour in one direction through DeKalb Avenue station during the rush period when it should be possible, if the City would carry out its contract, for this Company to operate at least 90 trains per hour during the rush periods in the morning and evening.

WHY DEKALB AVENUE IS CONGESTED

The reasons for the DeKalb Avenue congestion are self-evident. While sixteen tracks now feed into this station, directly or indirectly, from Brooklyn there are only six tracks of outlet to Manhattan. Two lines pass through Willoughby Street via Montague Street tunnel, Whitehall and Church Streets, Manhattan, to the Broadway subway. Four tracks pass over the Manhattan Bridge, two going through Canal Street to a connection with the Broadway subway and two joining the Centre Street loop, terminating at Chambers Street station.

ORIGINAL PLANS NOT CARRIED OUT

Now, the important fact about this situation and the connecting link between Ashland Place and the Nassau-

Broad Street Extension is that Contract 4 provided that these two tracks instead of forming a dam at Chambers Street should continue down Nassau and Broad Streets to a connection with the Whitehall-Montague tunnel and with the extra tracks in Broad Street for a terminal. This was an integral part of the system planned for operation by the Brooklyn Company so as to provide for double loop operation via Manhattan Bridge and the tunnel. Its absence today constitutes serious limitation on the capacity of the lines already built in Brooklyn and now in operation. It renders the two south tracks on Manhattan Bridge practically useless. It limits the number of trains through DeKalb Avenue, for the sixteen tracks of the various branches feeding into this station have, as a practical matter, only four tracks outlet to Manhattan. This in turn limits the number of trains and increases the interval between trains on the various branches.

THE WAY OUT OF DEKALB AVENUE CONGESTION

With these conditions existing it would only multiply the congestion and the blockades to attempt to route additional trains via Ashland Place into DeKalb Avenue. The completion and operation of the Nassau Street Line by allowing the use of the two south tracks on Manhattan Bridge and by the additional tracks on Broad Street would provide for an increase of approximately 50 per cent more trains through DeKalb Avenue station. A 50 per cent increase in service through DeKalb Avenue would be a Godsend not only to the people of Central Brooklyn and East New York and to the people who desire the Ashland Place Connection, but to the whole of South Brooklyn.

Transit Truths

While the directors at this time emphasize the importance and the inter-relationship of the 14th Street-Eastern, the Nassau-Broad Street Lines, and the Ashland Place Connection, they are not by any means minimizing the importance of the City living up to its contract to lengthen station platforms where necessary to accommodate full length trains and providing car shops, and the necessity for the Brooklyn Crosstown and the Washington Heights Lines or the need of another tunnel to Manhattan.

The Way Is Clear

The program which we now propose, however, is one which can be acted upon at once by the City. As far as the first two planks are concerned contracts are now in force. As far as the Ashland Place Connection is concerned this Company is ready to confer with public bodies or officials and to sign agreements such as were tentatively agreed upon by Commissioner Delaney and the Receiver for the predecessor of this Company in 1920 as soon as satisfactory assurance is given that the City will proceed with the construction and completion of the 14th Street-Eastern and Nassau Street Lines.

This is the short cut to Better Metropolitan Transit.

EDITORIAL OPINION

"The proposals of the B. M. T. deserve the most generous consideration by the City," said the Brooklyn Daily *Eagle* on December 18, 1923, the day the "Short Cut to Better Metropolitan Transit" was announced. "Mr. Dahl's report of today," the Brooklyn *Standard Union* declared, "is truly a report of progress."

Short Cut to Better Metropolitan Transit

"The daily flood" of subway passengers, observed the *New York Evening Post,* "threatens to burst the dike at a dozen points" so that the proposals made by the B. M. T., "eventually will mean much to central Brooklyn and East New York."

"The new management of the B. M. T. is to be commended for a correct understanding of the obligation on which it holds its charter; the public is to be congratulated on a sense of broad obligation on the part of the railroad officials which augurs for a much better condition of service in the future," said the Brooklyn Daily *Times.* On Friday, December 21, the New York *World* after referring to the Canal Street congestion as the most dangerous in the subway system, added that "the plans of the engineers of the Transit Commission should speedily be completed." The New York *Tribune* asserted that if the City did not begin construction "no admittance" signs would soon have to be posted in the subway entrance during rush hours. The Brooklyn *Citizen,* in an editorial on December 19, stressed the fact that while the companies had lived up to their obligations under the dual contracts by charging only a five cent fare the City had defaulted by not building the lines and shops and yards which it was obligated to construct under the same contract.

Despite this unanimity of editorial opinion, however, the City continued its political policy of obstruction and delay.

Chapter IV.
Transit Fares in Other Cities

OF the 288 cities in the United States now having a population of 25,000 or more, only twelve still retain the original five cent street car fare. The fare increases in the other 276 cities range from the elimination of reduced rate tickets—costing less than five cents per ride, to a ten cent cash fare.

In May, 1924, the Very Rev. Monsignor John L. Belford, D.D., one of the leading Catholic prelates of Brooklyn, in a public address before the Jamaica Board of Trade, said:

"Why have we not more subways? There is just one reason. Men will not invest in a losing business. Make it worth while and you will have all the subways you need. Allow the B. M. T. and the I. R. T. to charge 7 or 8 cents and you will get more subways and you will get them quick.

"If it costs a farmer 49 cents a dozen to produce a dozen eggs, you cannot ask him to sell them for 45 cents.

"The laborer is worthy of his hire, be he an individual or a corporation."

With Monsignor Belford's permission, excerpts from this statement were published in the *Look Ahead* bulletin in our cars. On Sunday, June 8, 1924, I issued a statement to the press on transit fares in other cities, as follows:

"The posting of a bulletin in our cars quoting a public statement made by Monsignor John L. Belford, D.D., of Brooklyn, coupled with the public demands of the people of the Bronx and Queens for bus and surface car service even if the fare is more than five cents, has inspired a large number of inquiries as to the attitude of the B. M. T.

"Briefly, this Company ever since its organization one year ago, has maintained that it can live on a five cent fare. But, there is a vast difference between living on bread and water and living on a square meal. We are today providing a service on our rapid transit lines which, if the taxpayers of this city and the investors were receiving a fair return on the money invested in our rapid transit lines, would cost 7.31 cents per passenger. As long as the taxpayers and investors are willing to hold the bag we can give 7.31 cent service for five cents, but we cannot afford to give 7½ cent or 8 cent service. We are today maintaining a maximum service on our rapid transit lines and there is no possibility of this service being increased until the City completes the Fourteenth Street-Eastern Line and the Nassau-Broad Street Extension and builds the new shops and yards which it is obligated to construct under Contract 4.

"To accuse the B. M. T. of agitating for an increased fare is nothing more than an attempt to pull wool over the eyes of the people of this city. This Company does not need a higher fare half as much as the taxpayers do. The taxpayers are the real losers in this community. They have $250,000,000 invested in rapid transit lines —investments made by the City of New York. This money is tied up. The City is receiving no return on this gigantic investment. If, however, the car riders today were paying the cost of service the City could borrow all the money it needs to build all the transit lines the people of this city demand and investors would will-

Transit Truths

ingly come forward with all the money needed for the equipment and operation of these lines.

"New York is today practically the only metropolis in the United States where its city officials will not look the facts in the face. In Detroit and Seattle, where the transit lines are owned and operated by the municipal authorities the fares were increased from five cents to six and ten cents respectively. In Indianapolis, Baltimore and Providence, the street railway fares have only recently been increased because the private operating companies could not continue service without an increased revenue. So that today the cash fare rates in nineteen large cities throughout the country, compared to 1913 are as follows:

	1913	1924
Chicago	5	10-7
Philadelphia	5	7-8*
Detroit — Municipal operation today		6
Private operation	5	
Cleveland	3	6
St. Louis	5	7
Boston	5	10
Baltimore	5	8
Buffalo	5	7
Pittsburgh	5	10
Washington, D. C.	5	8
Indianapolis	5	7
Seattle — Municipal operation today		10
Private operation	5	
Richmond, Va.	5	6

* On September 20, 1924 the fare was increased to 8 cents, or two tickets for fifteen cents.

Transit Fares in Other Cities

Dallas, Texas	5	6
Omaha	5	7
Kansas City	5	8
Toledo	5	8
Cincinnati	5	9
Providence	5	8

"In September, 1923, Detroit, which had up to that time been one of the exhibition cities of the five cent fare, found it expedient to increase the fare to six cents in order to keep up with the costs of operation. Detroit was followed three months later by a similar increase in Cleveland. Detroit is the largest city in the United States where street railway lines are operated by the municipal authorities. It is a notable fact that it was only after the lines had been taken over by the City that the fare increase was put into effect.

"Until the lines were acquired by the City in 1922, a private company operated on a five cent fare. On May 15, 1922, the City purchased the lines and property of the Detroit Electric Railway Company and operated on a five cent fare for one year and four months. In the Fall of 1923, the rate was increased to six cents despite the fact that under City ownership the Company enjoys material advantages in taxes, being exempt from federal taxation and income taxes; from school, park, franchise and street lighting taxes; from the payment of car and track licenses and any tax for the support of public service commissions or other state regulatory bodies, and is exempted from operating suburban lines that do not pay.

"The primary theory of municipal operation—that it will provide lower fares than privately operated companies can give—has failed to work out in practice in Detroit.

"Political interference with fares and the operation of

electric railways in Seattle brought about an actual money loss of about $500,000 between March 1 and June 15, 1923.

"Under private operation the street railway lines in Seattle were operated on a five cent fare. In order to continue operating and making needed extensions, the Company petitioned for a fare increase from five to seven cents. The petition was not granted and the municipal authorities bought the lines. In the following year, under municipal operation, the fare rate was increased to ten cents. After the lines had been operating for three years at a ten cent fare and breaking even, the same city authorities who had caused the City to refuse the petition of the private owners, caused the five cent fare to be reinstalled in March, 1923, insisting that a nickel fare was sufficient for any street car line and that it would attract more business than a higher fare. The losses in three months were so great that in June, 1923, the ten cent fare was restored.

"In an editorial on the situation the Tacoma *News-Tribune* wrote:

"'Mayor Edward J. Brown of Seattle, pledged the people a five cent fare when he was elected to office. He gave it to them along with an unannounced deficit of $5,000 per day which home-owners must pay in taxes. . . . Mayor Brown's action is frankly dictated by political expediency. His eyes are on the Democratic nomination for governor, and the five cent plank was to be the stepping stone to let him in. The $5,000 deficit unkindly obtruded itself but he hopes to keep his record clear technically and depends upon the notoriously short memory of voters.'

"As this is not an era of transit miracles New York can hardly be expected to escape the experience of the people in other cities."

Are Public Servants "Worthy of Their Hire"?

BY authorizing the N. Y. & Queens County Railway Company to charge a six-cent fare, the Transit Commission recognized a fundamental principle of civic justice. Public servants, be they city officials or transit companies which serve the public, are "worthy of their hire."

In more than 545 cities transit fares range from 6 cents to 10 cents

Because the people as well as the city officials know, as a result of years of experience, that transit service today costs more than it did in 1913 and that adequate service cannot be maintained without an adequate fare.

During the past three months transit fares have been increased in thirty cities, including Washington, D. C., Baltimore and Indianapolis.

Fares in Leading Cities:

	1913	TODAY		1913	TODAY
Chicago	5	10-7	Indianapolis	5	7
Philadelphia	5	7	Seattle	5	10
Detroit	5	6	Richmond, Va.	5	6
Cleveland	3	6	Dallas, Tex.	5	6
St. Louis	5	7	Omaha	5	7
Boston	5	10	Kansas City	5	8
Baltimore	5	8	Toledo	5	8
Buffalo	5	7	Cincinnati	5	9
Pittsburgh	5	10	Providence	5	8
Washington, D. C.	5	8	Denver	5	8

20% Increase in Queens

The increase in fare on the N.Y. & Queens County Railway Company was necessary because of the increased cost of materials and wages; otherwise the Company would have been forced to stop service. The increase from 5 cents to 6 cents is but a 20 per cent increase.

66⅔% Increase in Mayor Hylan's Salary

On May 23, 1923, Mayor Hylan signed the bill increasing his salary from $15,000 to $25,000, an increase of 66-2/3 per cent. At that time the Mayor refused to make a public statement, but the New York AMERICAN said that public servants were "worthy of their hire."

This is as true of a public servant transit company as it is of a public servant in any city office.

Although the Brooklyn-Manhattan Transit Corporation has no financial interest in the New York & Queens County Railway Company, the B.-M. T. believes that it has a two-fold public duty: 1. To provide the best possible service on all its lines under the present conditions and restrictions; and, 2, to give the public all the FACTS known to the company or its directors on the biggest problem facing the people of this city—How can New York City obtain adequate transit?

GERHARD M. DAHL, Chairman
BROOKLYN-MANHATTAN TRANSIT CORPORATION.

Chapter V.
Challenge to Debate

AFTER the advertisement: "Are Public Servants Worthy of Their Hire?" appeared in the leading newspapers, I challenged Mayor Hylan to a public debate in the following communication:

Brooklyn-Manhattan Transit Corporation
85 Clinton Street
Brooklyn, N. Y.

August 4, 1924

Hon. John F. Hylan,
Mayor, City of New York,
City Hall, New York City.

Dear Sir:—

Returning today from ten days' absence, my attention is called to your letter of July 31st to Chairman John H. Delaney in which you indulge in insinuations with reference to me. You say, "You may be surprised to learn that Mr. Dahl of the B. M. T. went to French Lick to see some politicians who he thought might be able to 'reach' me."

That statement is unqualifiedly untrue. Whether you knew it was untrue when you made it, I do not know.

It is not the first time you have published calculated innuendoes. On June 9th there was published in the daily press a statement by you in which you said, among other

[52]

Challenge to Debate

things, "Dahl personally conferred with men very close to me in an endeavor to get these men to induce me to allow the B. M. T. to increase its fare; also to put over the proposed Crosstown Line tying up at both ends with the B. M. T."

Immediately after you made that statement, I denied it at a public luncheon in Brooklyn. I repeat the denial. Your statement of June 9th is also unqualifiedly untrue. In my public statement in Brooklyn, I gave you credit for sincerity in making the statement of June 9th saying that while your statement was inaccurate, I assumed that someone had so informed you and that you made the statement in good faith. I now withdraw the credit I gave you for sincerity and good faith.

You have on two different occasions stated that I talked with certain men. You have not named the men. You have not repeated what I am supposed to have said. You have sought to convey the impression of impropriety on my part without having sufficient courage to boldly make those misrepresentations which you attempt to convey by innuendo.

It is true that I have talked to many people about the transit situation since I became Chairman of the B. M. T. It is true that among the people I have talked to are some of your friends. It is true that I have constantly emphasized the deplorable conditions and our desire to help remedy them and my conviction that you personally are responsible for those conditions and that you personally must be ignorant both of the facts with reference to transit conditions and of the sound economic principles which should be applied in order to remedy the existing situation. It is also true that I have tried to talk to you personally without success. You will recall that we met at a luncheon in May, during which we had a very brief conversation and touched only slightly on the transit situation. You will recall that under date of May 20th I wrote you as follows:

"It was a great personal pleasure to meet you last Saturday at luncheon and I shall be grateful for an opportunity to continue the very brief conversation we had at that time. I have given a great deal of time and study to the transit situation in New York and I have in mind some constructive ideas which seem to me helpful and practical and which I should like to discuss with you. If you can spare the time, I shall be glad to call and go over the situation with you. Any time next Tuesday or Wednesday would be entirely convenient for me, but if you wish to fix some other hour, I will arrange my appointments accordingly."

Notwithstanding the urgency of transit relief; notwithstanding my offer of assistance and my sincere effort to contribute something to the sound solution of this problem, you did not even show me the courtesy of a reply.

For seven years you have been misleading and fooling the people in this community who actually ride on the subways. For seven years you have blocked every effort at transit relief. You, and only you are to blame for the present congestion in our subways and the present deplorable condition of the whole transit situation. You have used the transit situation as a political escalator. You have been willing to sacrifice the comfort, the convenience and even the necessities of the people of this community to your selfish political interests. You are persisting in that course.

In order that the public may be fully informed as to

Challenge to Debate

the unsoundness of your position and the measure of your responsibility I shall be glad to meet you personally and publicly discuss the whole transit situation and give you an opportunity to defend your position. If you will name a date and hall in Greater New York, I will hire the hall and be there to meet you on any evening you may suggest on condition that each of us may appoint a representative so that they may agree upon the division of time and tickets and other details. Furthermore, I ask you to bring with you to that meeting—if you have the courage to accept my invitation—the "friends" you vaguely describe in your letter of June 9th and whom you dare not name and the "politicians" whom you mention in your letter of July 31st to Chairman Delaney and whom you dare not name, and give me an opportunity to meet them face to face.

The only arguments you make in the transit situation are those of personal abuse. I am aware that anyone who opposes or differs with you on any matter whatsoever incurs your personal resentment and that you adopt prompt methods no matter how unscrupulous in an attempt to silence them and, at the same time, to impress upon others the danger of disagreeing with you. After all, however, we are still living in an age of free speech and I believe that my duty and responsibility as Chairman of the B. M. T. compels me to acquaint the public with the facts even though I thereby run the risk of being persecuted personally by you.

Yours truly,

(Signed)   GERHARD M. DAHL.

Following the publication of this letter the Brooklyn Daily *Eagle* said:

"The Mayor has capitalized the transit situation for seven years or more. His attacks upon the transit companies have been his chief political asset and his promises of relief were the bait he held out to the voters to secure their support. The issue today is over those promises. The promised relief has not been forthcoming."

Chapter VI.
Build More Transit Lines

THE western half of the 14th Street Line, extending from Sixth Avenue and 14th Street, Manhattan, under the East River to Montrose Avenue, Brooklyn, was opened on June 30, 1924. The first train from New York to Brooklyn was operated by Chairman McAneny of the Transit Commission and Mayor Hylan ran the train on the return trip. Upon this occasion Mayor Hylan and representatives of the B. M. T., spoke to civic organizations from the same platform.

On the following day the new Board of Transportation, authorized by the last Legislature, was appointed by the Mayor. As full power to build subway lines was lodged by law in this board and as the Hon. John H. Delaney was appointed Chairman I wrote to him on July 12th, offering him and his associates the full co-operation of the B. M. T.

In a public statement issued on July 14th when the letter to Chairman Delaney was made public, I declared that there were two transit issues facing the public:

1. How and when can the crowded conditions and crowded service be relieved, and,

2. How can the public obtain adequate service at the lowest cost?

Concluding my statement I said that "the best policy for New York City today is: Universal service with one fare."

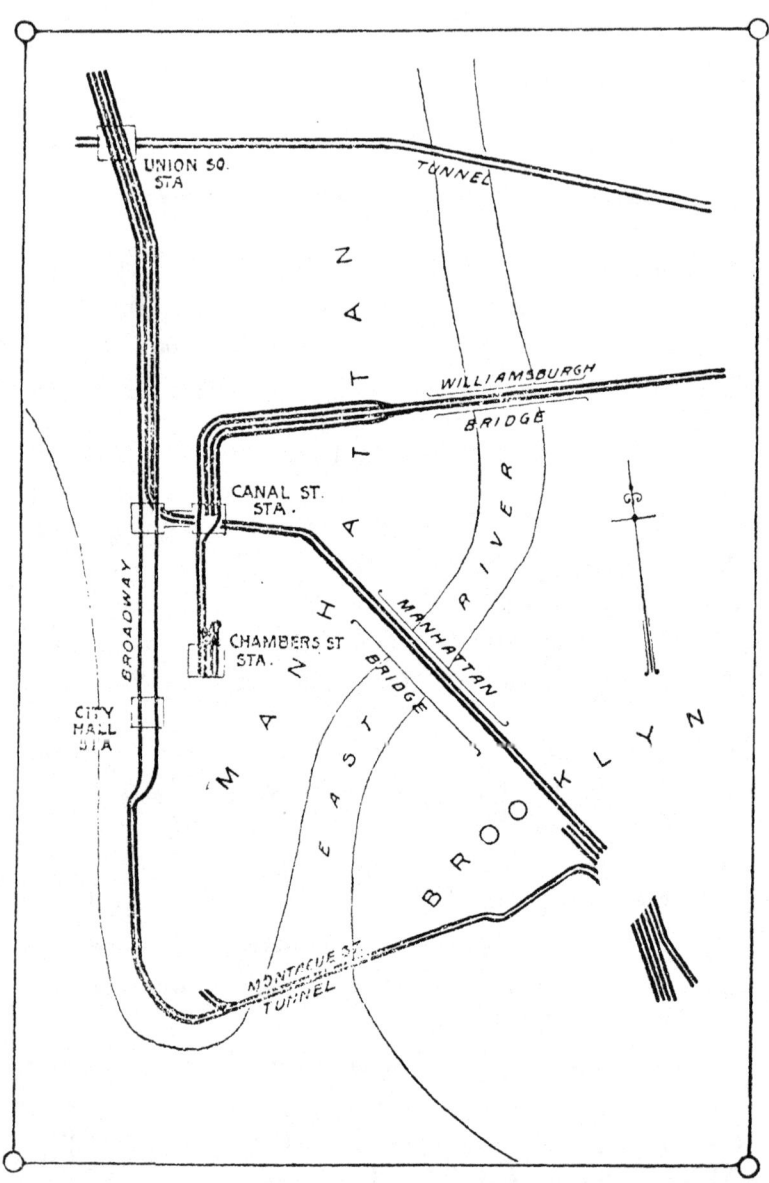

Build More Transit Lines

"If the City authorities desire to construct independent lines and duplicate fares," the statement added, "the B. M. T. has nothing whatsoever to lose. All the losses will fall upon the car riders who will have to pay two or more fares if they use two or more lines, and upon the taxpayers and rent payers who will have to bear the cost of construction, if the new lines are not operated at a profit."

Because the letter to Chairman Delaney was an attempt to clarify all the transit questions pending at the time between the Board of Transportation and the Company, with the exception of shops and yards, I am including it herewith:

> New York Rapid Transit Corporation
> 85 Clinton Street
> Brooklyn, N. Y.
>
> July 12, 1924

To the Board of Transportation,
49 Lafayette Street,
New York, N. Y.

Sirs:—

This Company, as the present contracting party with the City of New York under Rapid Transit Contract 4 and related certificates, desires to call certain matters to your attention in view of the jurisdiction conferred upon your board by Chapter 573 of the Laws of 1924. It is assumed that, because of public need, you will take under early consideration possible additional transit facilities. There has already been very considerable public discussion of possible new routes. In addition this Company has pointed out to your predecessor, the Transit

Commission, the need of completing the lines contemplated under Contract 4. It is hoped, therefore, that it will not be regarded as out of place if this Company now indicates to you its position on various transit questions so that you may have them before you in an early consideration of transit problems.

WAR INCREASED COSTS

The Transit Commission, within the last year, submitted to the Board of Estimate the so-called Washington Heights and Brooklyn Crosstown routes for which there appears to be general public demand and public need. Although the adoption of a route, under the Rapid Transit Act, does not require a determination, at that time, of the operator of the route when constructed, assertions have been made that this Company, directly or indirectly, has been promoting the idea that such routes should be so laid out and constructed that they must be operated by this Company as a part of its system. This is not an accurate statement of the point of view of this Company and for an obvious reason. Under Contract 4 this Company is obligated to carry passengers for a five cent fare the length of the system. Such a provision could have been agreed upon at the time the contract was made only on the theory that costs of operation would either remain stationary or decrease. The war, however, intervened and its attending results produced a scale of costs that continues. The predecessor of this Company was compelled, as a result, to go through a receivership and a reorganization. This Company was then organized on a financial basis that permits it to live on a five cent fare. This Company therefore can continue to fulfill its obligations under Contract 4 on the present fare. It cannot,

Build More Transit Lines

however, earn what it is justly entitled to under the contract, nor can anything be earned to pay the interest and amortization on the City's investment in the rapid transit lines operated by this Company. This Company, therefore, is not anxious to have additional lines added to be operated as a part of its system on the present fare provisions. Consequently, any statement from whatever source, may be regarded as inaccurate that this Company, or its related companies, is directly or indirectly, seeking to have these two proposed routes, or any other new routes, linked up as a part of its system under existing contractual conditions.

ACCOUNTING SYSTEM

On the other hand, this Company is alive to its public duties and obligations under Contract No. 4 and related certificates. That contract provided for the construction of certain lines by the City and their operation as a unified system. While the lines thus to be constructed represented a very great increase in the then transit facilities of the City, it was realized that they did not represent all the future facilities that the city would require, and, although the contracts were made in 1913, the need of further facilities has been obviously apparent for several years past. Consequently, in an attempt to provide for the future, the contracts contain provisions on extensions under which if the City lays out and constructs a new rapid transit line as an extension to the lines under the contract the City may require the Company to operate such extension as a part of its system. As to accounting, the Company, however, may elect to operate such extension either as a part of the system pool or on a separate accounting. Under the latter, the City is obliged to assume any financial losses resulting from the operation of such extension. Under these pro-

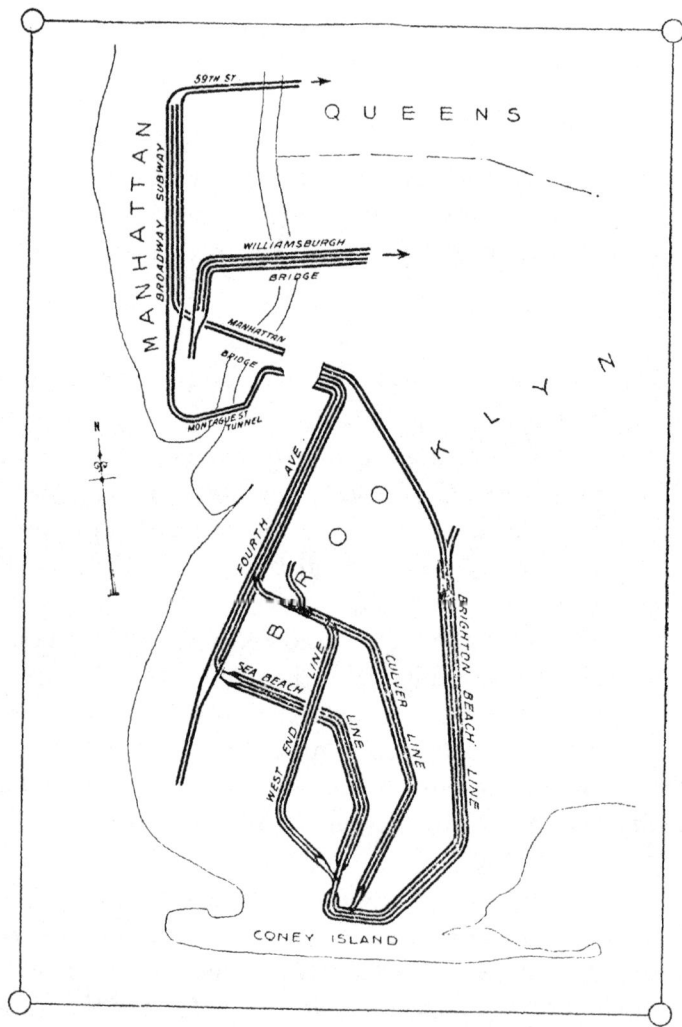

Build More Transit Lines

visions as to extensions, the City has the option, as to a new line, either to construct it so as to be operatable as part of this system or of another system or independently. On the other hand this Company has no option as to the route or construction of a line and must operate it, if built as an extension to this system, but it has an option, in such case, on accounting.

BENEFITS OF LARGE SYSTEM

Those provisions as to extensions were insisted upon by representatives of the City, doubtless because it suited public convenience best to have unification of rapid transit facilities rather than from time to time the introduction into the city of independent systems with a separate fare on each. It seemed only fair, that, if at the time agreement was being made as to lines then to be constructed, the Company should also agree to operate extensions in order that the public living along such extensions might have the benefit of unification with the existing system and thereby be put on a parity with communities already enjoying the benefit of the facilities of a large system.

MAXIMUM CONSTRUCTION NEEDED

This Company is mindful of the public duty thus assumed to operate extensions to its system if built by the City. Its position therefore is this, that, while it is not urged that new routes should be laid out and constructed as extensions to its system, nevertheless it believes that new facilities are needed, and that if the City, through your board, should lay out and construct new routes as extensions to its system and direct, under the provisions of Contract 4, this Company to equip and operate them, this Company will equip them with its own capital and operate them as a part of its system under the contract. It takes this attitude because of its contractual duties and its desire to recognize the increased benefit to the public arising from unification of operation. It also recognizes that with the same amount of public investment more transit facilities can be provided if used to build extensions to this system than if used to build and equip a system to be operated independently, either by the City or otherwise. Public requirements of additional facilities call for maximum construction at the earliest moment.

THE CITY'S OBLIGATIONS

This Company thus desires to make clear its attitude on the construction and operation of new routes. Reference has already been made to the provisions of Contract 4 in respect to lines and facilities to be built by the City and by the Company. This Company, and its predecessors, have constructed the facilities that it contracted to provide and for which it has obtained approval. It has in operation such facilities as well as the lines completed by the City and is operating them as a unified system under the five cent fare provisions of the contract although the City has not carried out its end of the contract to construct all the lines and facilities to which it obligated itself on condition that the Company would do its share. The Company has fulfilled, on a five cent fare, to the best of its ability with the incomplete facilities furnished by the City. It is ordinarily expected that contracts entered into will be fulfilled on both sides. For that reason, therefore, this Company is obligated to itself, its investors and the public whom it serves to direct your attention, thus early upon your entry into your official

Build More Transit Lines

duties, to the important obligations of the City that have not been fulfilled.

These obligations are the completion of the 14th Street Line, the construction of the Nassau-Broad Street connection, the construction of shops and yards and the lengthening of station platforms.

CANAL STREET CONGESTION

The 14th Street Line and Nassau Line were important parts of the system to which this Company agreed and they are essential to rendering of proper service on the lines now in operation in Brooklyn and Queens. Failure to complete these lines for operation has resulted in the disgraceful and dangerous congestion that occurs at Canal Street station every morning and evening of the week and year and has existed for years and must continue for the period of years necessary to construct these lines unless your board or the Transit Commission can devise or suggest some form of immediate relief that has not occurred to this Company.

As to the 14th Street Line, the subway portion, completed some years ago under contracts let in 1915, was put in operation on June 30, 1924, as a shuttle line. The remainder of the line was, under the provisions of Contract 4, to be elevated construction. The Transit Commission, however, at the suggestion of city authorities, asked the attitude of this Company upon a proposed modification of the contract so as to provide for underground construction. This Company replied that it would agree to the modification suggested provided certain physical conditions could be met. It thus replied in the hopes that thereby definite steps would be taken towards actual construction. It is still willing to agree

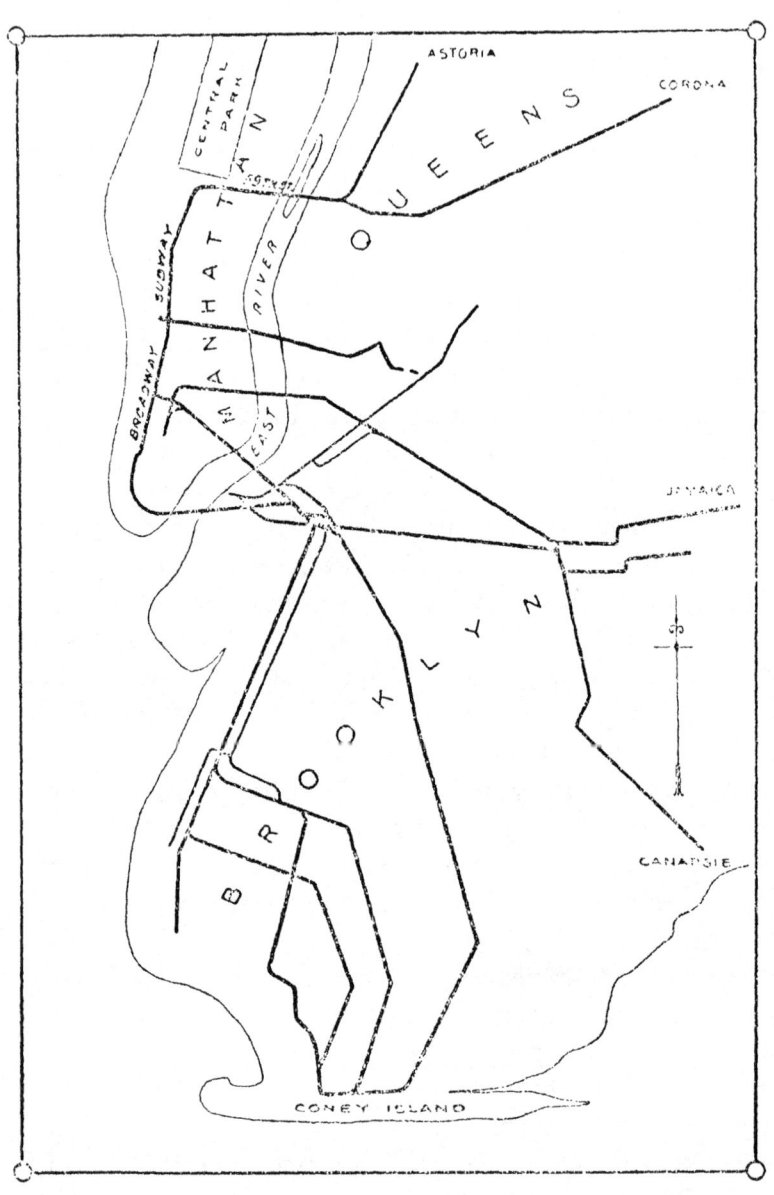

Build More Transit Lines

to a modification to a subway as outlined to your predecessor. It is also aware that a subway, if begun, will sometime be completed. And conditions at Canal Street are such that relief must be provided. The completion of the 14th Street to East New York, with proper connection, and of the Nassau-Broad Line will allow a large diversion of travel that now congests the Broadway elevated and the Centre Street loop and creates abnormal and dangerous crowding and transferring at Broadway and Canal Street.

DeKalb Avenue Station

The Nassau-Broad Street Line with terminal facilities in Broad Street will furnish the loop operation contemplated in and expected from Contract 4. Service in Brooklyn is largely limited by the capacity of the DeKalb Avenue station. This station has 16 tracks feeding into it to and from the 4th Avenue system and the Brighton Beach, with only four tracks to Manhattan, two over the Manhattan Bridge and two through the Montague Street tunnel. There are two additional tracks on Manhattan Bridge leading to the Chambers Street station that cannot be used for Brooklyn service because of the effort to accommodate the travel through Canal Street coming over the Williamsburg Bridge. In maximum service this Company cannot, therefore, get through the DeKalb Avenue station more than 60 trains per hour which must be apportioned to the various lines that connect with this station and that could accommodate and should have more trains if they could be operated though this station. The completed 14th Street Line would relieve Canal Street and the Nassau-Broad Line would allow loop operation with full use of the four tracks on the Manhattan Bridge and thus permit approximately 90 trains, or 50% increase, to be operated through DeKalb Avenue station with corresponding increase on each of the outlying lines. These two uncompleted sections, 14th Street and Nassau-Broad, are, therefore, not mere local facilities for a particular locality. They are links that will permit very substantial improvement and increase in service to every part of the system operated by this Company. Failure to complete them means a continuing increased cost of operation to this Company not justified under the contract nor considered as a normal part of cost of operation under the five cent fare. Failure to complete them also means continuing congestion and inconvenience to the public.

CONSTRUCTION NEEDED

This Company is keenly sensitive to the limitations, imposed by failure to construct these links, upon its ability to increase the service to the growing sections of Brooklyn and Queens, and it would be remiss in its public duty if it failed again to urge the proper public officers to give first consideration to the early construction of these links both because the City obligated itself eleven years ago by contract to construct them promptly and because they are urgently needed to furnish the increased service that the public has a right to expect. They will, therefore, provide more facilities than could be now afforded by equal expenditures upon any other line. From the point of view of maximum additional facilities, and also from a realization of the moral and legal obligations of the City, it would appear that, if the City is limited in its financial resources, these links should be given consideration, along with shops, yards

Build More Transit Lines

and station lengthening, ahead of any proposed new route.

It would seem unnecessary to explain the importance of shops and yards adequate to maintain properly the equipment operated upon and under the requirements of a rapid transit system. Yet they have not been provided by the City. The Company has, in consequence, been compelled to maintain and care for its equipment under conditions difficult and more expensive than contemplated by Contract 4. It is natural, therefore, to expect that you will desire to give early consideration to the construction of shops and yards so that equipment may, adequately, efficiently and economically, be maintained to that high degree that the public has a right to expect.

Full Length Trains

Existing facilities are inadequate even for the maintenance of existing equipment except by unusual exertion. They are, therefore, as to an increase in equipment, a barrier that should be removed in order that additional equipment may be obtained and utilized as needed.

The contract and plans contemplated full length trains. Unfortunately, however, many stations are too short to allow full train operation which would permit at least 15% increase in rush hour service. If the Company is to furnish full train operation as contemplated, provision must be made by the City for lengthening station platforms.

This Company, under existing limitations, is endeavoring to improve its service wherever possible and to maintain and increase its equipment in order that it may fulfill its duties to the public. It is endeavoring and desires to earn the confidence of the public that it is giving the best service possible and that it is diligent in seeking further means of improving transportation upon which the distribution of population and industry, and, therefore, the prosperity of all the boroughs, is dependent.

Reference has been made herein to possible limitations on the debt capacity of the City and to provisions of Contract 4 that handicap the Company and serve to restrict consideration of comprehensive transit plans. This Company will be glad to consider from your board or from the Transit Commission any suggestions looking towards a revision of Contract 4 and related certificates bearing upon the bases of present or future operations or expansion. While this Company will continue to fulfill its duties under that contract and insist upon compliance with obligations undertaken therein by the City, it is entirely willing to give consideration to a new basis of relation between the City and the Company, whether relating to present contractual conditions or future routes or the means whereby new capital may be available for comprehensive construction.

Relative to the matters to which reference herein has been made, as well as any other under the jurisdiction of your board, this Company will be glad to give any expressions from your board prompt and careful consideration and will be glad to have its officers and representatives confer thereon with your board or its representatives at any time in order that transit relief may be accomplished without loss of time.

        Respectfully,

            GERHARD M. DAHL, *Chairman,*
            New York Rapid Transit Corporation.

Build More Transit Lines

If the attitude of the New York newspapers is an indication of public sentiment the editorials which were written following the publication of this letter would seem to indicate that "the Brooklyn-Manhattan Transit Corporation has gone more than half way along the road to better service," to quote from the New York *Bulletin,* a Democratic newspaper. The New York *Times* said that "every dollar spent on these obligations [those recorded in the letter above] would multiply itself." The Brooklyn *Times* declared "that there is an earnest desire upon the part of the public for subway construction.... The City authorities should take notice of this demand."

Although by this time even the Democratic newspapers despaired of constructive action by Mayor Hylan they had faith in Chairman Delaney.

"Failure to live up to contracts," averred the Brooklyn Daily *Eagle,* "is merely a characteristic of the Hylan program of transit improvements. . . . As Mr. Dahl very well knows, the crying need in this City is for more subways. Last summer Mayor Hylan made a verbal contract with the citizens of Brooklyn and Manhattan to build a crosstown line. Last spring Mayor Hylan breached the contract. If he would do that with his people what would he not do with a contract made with the wicked 'interests'?

"Fortunately, however," the *Eagle* concluded, "the City's transit problems are now placed in the hands of a Board of Transportation."

But, whatever may be the attitude of individual city officials they lose their independence of action and freedom of thought on transit under Mayor Hylan. In order to register this fact upon the public mind I authorized the insertion of the following page advertisement in the leading daily and weekly newspapers of Brooklyn, Queens, Richmond, the Bronx and Manhattan:

WHICH WILL IT BE?

Delaney and Dig? OR Delaney and Delay?

On May 26, 1919, Governor Smith appointed the Hon. John H. Delaney Transit Construction Commissioner. On August 18, 1920, Mr. Delaney wrote the following letter:

"It is my intention to press forward with all speed possible the completion of all lines included in the Dual Subway Contracts, and specifically the Nassau Street line as well as the others.

"The engineers have begun work on the preliminary sketches for the Nassau Street line. The Fourteenth Street-Eastern District line will be given preference, however, as we hope to have that ready for the preparation of contracts before the end of this year."

Why did Chairman Delaney promise "speed" in 1920 and then decide upon delay in 1924?

There is only one reason. In 1920, under Governor Smith, he was a free official whose word was as good as his bond. He could make pledges in the public interest and urge the city to fulfill them.

Today, under Mayor Hylan, he is forced to break his official promises?

On July 1, 1924, the Hon. John H. Delaney was appointed Chairman of the Board of Transportation by Mayor Hylan. On August 16, 1924, he made the following public statement:

"... the building of the Nassau Street line may be deferred for some time, there being some question on the part of the City concerning its obligation to build, which must be settled by litigation."

On August 22, 1924, Mr. Delaney repeated: "We will not make any effort to build this line unless the Courts compel us to do so."

Here are 8 reasons why *Chairman Delaney was right in 1920* when he promised to complete the Nassau and 14th Street Eastern Lines.

1. It will permit the B. M. T. to run 30 more *trains* per hour during rush periods;
2. The work can be completed in three years at a cost of $11,000,000. No other subway construction work can be completed in this time or at this cost which will provide anything like the same amount of additional transportation facilities.
3. This will increase the maximum service through DeKalb Avenue station from Brooklyn at least 50% to Lower Manhattan and through Times Square;
4. The increased service will be available immediately to all passengers on the Fourth Avenue, Sea Beach, West End, Culver and Brighton lines;
5. It will provide another trunk line through Lower Manhattan;
6. Completion of the Nassau and the Fourteenth Street lines to East New York will practically eliminate the necessity for transfers at Canal Street during the rush hour when 50,000 car-riders have to walk two city blocks across busy streets to get to and from their trains;
7. The B. M. T. will be able to increase the number of steel cars;
8. In addition, the City has the money; the plans are ready; and the City, on March 19, 1913, CONTRACTED TO BUILD THE NASSAU LINE.

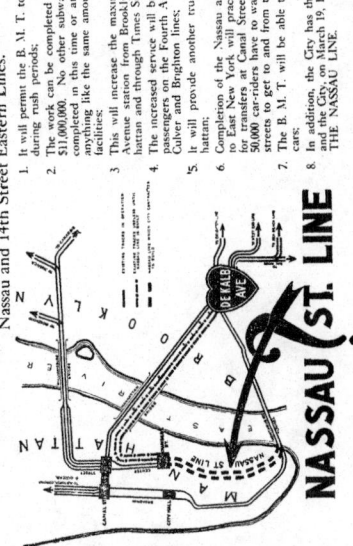

"Delaney and Dig" is a *real constructive policy*. Support it!
"Delaney and Delay" is a Hylan policy. Defeat it!

Is it not in the interest of the people of Brooklyn to urge Chairman Delaney to "speed" the construction of this line?
If the people of Brooklyn and East New York really want transit relief *now*, here is their opportunity. Nassau is the short cut to better service.

GERHARD M. DAHL, Chairman,
Brooklyn-Manhattan Transit Corporation,
85 Clinton St., Brooklyn.

Chapter VII.
Employees Stock Ownership

TODAY eight out of every ten employees of the B. M. T. Lines own from one to three shares of the Company's preferred stock. As a result of their subscriptions 26,000 persons are today stockholders of the B. M. T., including besides the employees, 16,000 individuals and banks and insurance companies and the United States Government.

In making announcement of the stock ownership plan to the employees and the public the following statements were issued by William S. Menden, President of the B. M. T.

>Brooklyn-Manhattan Transit Corporation
>85 Clinton Street
>Brooklyn, N. Y.
>
>July 16, 1924.

To Fellow Employees:

During the past several months a considerable number of employees have expressed to me a desire to have the B. M. T. Companies provide an arrangement under which employees might become stockholders under some plan similar to that adopted by other large corporations. I heartily approve of such a plan, and the directors at our request have approved a plan as outlined in the enclosed circular.

This plan will permit employees purchasing a limited number of shares of stock on the basis of monthly or weekly payments, and at the same time any dividends declared on this stock will accrue to the account of the employee stockholder. The arrangement specifically permits the employee at any time within twelve months (the date of final instalment) to cancel his or her subscription, and the Company agrees in this event to return to the subscriber all payments previously made by such subscriber plus interest at the rate of 5%.

I believe that the plan as now offered is such that every employee is justified in becoming a subscriber and a stockholder of the Company.

The details of the subscription plan will be presented to you by those having charge of the work in the various departments.

W. S. MENDEN, *President.*

BROOKLYN-MANHATTAN TRANSIT CORPORATION
85 CLINTON STREET, BROOKLYN, NEW YORK

To Employees:

THIS CORPORATION, for itself and its subsidiary companies, has acquired voting trust certificates for fifteen thousand shares of its issued and outstanding Preferred Stock (Series A, carrying dividends at the rate of $6 per share per annum payable quarterly) for the purpose of making this offer to our employees on what we believe to be attractive terms.

Terms of Offer. Therefore, on behalf of itself and its subsidiaries, the Brooklyn-Manhattan Transit Corporation hereby offers to the employees of this system the right to subscribe for said fifteen thousand shares at $65 per share, payable $5 on or before August 1, 1924, and $5 on or before the first of each succeeding month until fully paid. Interest will be charged at the rate of 5% per annum from August 1, 1924, on deferred payments and accrued dividends from July 1, 1924, will be credited as received.

Final Net Cost Approximately $60 Per Share. Any employee who completes final payment and retains ownership of his stock for one year thereafter will receive a one dollar refund on the subscription price and an additional one dollar refund if he retains ownership of his stock for two years after final payment. With such refunds, adjusting interest at 5% and crediting the full annual dividend to date of final payment, the net price for this stock to any employee retaining ownership for two years after final payment will be approximately $60 per share. With declared dividends of $6 per annum, this will represent a return of around 10% on such amount of investment.

Upon receipt of final payment, a voting trust certificate will be delivered to the subscriber without restriction and he will thereafter receive directly all dividends declared thereon.

Conditions—

Any employee of not less than three months' service may subscribe for *not more than ten shares* subject to acceptance by the Company with the right reserved to the Company to reduce subscriptions and allot shares so that every employee may subscribe for and receive at least one share.

At the request of any employee, the Company will deduct the instalments from his pay at the rate of $1.25 per week where he is paid weekly, or $5 per month where he is paid monthly.

Subscriptions may be cancelled at any time prior to final payment upon written notice to the Company, upon which the employee so cancelling his subscription will receive all payments made by him together with interest at the rate of 5% per annum on such payments.

The Company reserves the right to cancel any subscription and to make similar refund in case of failure to pay any instalment for more than ten days after it is due, and also, in case a subscriber under this offer ceases to be an employee of the Company before final payment has been made.

Prior to final payment the rights hereby offered are non-transferable except to another employee and then only with the consent of this Company.

All subscriptions under this offer must be filed with the Company on or before July 26, 1924.

W. S. MENDEN, *President,*
July 16, 1924.   Brooklyn-Manhattan Transit Corporation.

Chapter VIII.
Buses

ON July 23, 1924, the B. M. T. announced that it had purchased 10 large, modern double deck buses.

"We have purchased these buses," I said in a public statement, "in order that the public, as well as the public authorities if they deem it wise to authorize us to operate bus lines, may understand that we are in earnest in our desire to render the broadest possible service. Various sections have developed very rapidly during the last few years.

"Construction of rapid transit lines into such sections is practically impossible. Such lines would be extensions of existing trunk lines which are already overburdened. Logically, any rapid transit construction should be important trunk connections, such as 14th Street and Nassau, to allow fuller use in rush hours of existing facilities. Even in surface railroads further extensions will take time and need to be carefully considered. The conclusion is inevitable, therefore, that buses should play an important part, in a large system, in extending transportation into growing sections.

"It should not be overlooked that houses can be erected and occupied within a year and a new section thus largely populated without adequate transportation. The construction of rapid transit lines is a slow process, taking a good many years from the laying out of a route to the beginning of operation. This Company desires to do its part towards obtaining immediate transit for such sections and thus indirectly encouraging further development of outlying sections.

"Bus operation seems the logical and immediate method of furnishing such service."

After a trial period of operation by special hire, formal application was made to the Mayor and Board of Estimate and Apportionment for bus franchises in the following communication:

        Brooklyn-Manhattan Transit Corporation
                   85 Clinton Street
                   Brooklyn, N. Y.
                              August 13, 1924.

To the Mayor and Board of Estimate
of the City of New York,
City Hall.

Sirs:

After a careful consideration of bus operation this Company realizes that, in line with its duty to the public, served in general by B. M. T. Lines, buses should be operated, supplementary to existing transit lines. Due to the rapid growth of population and extensive residential developments there are now many sections beyond the convenient reach of existing lines. It is important that such development should not be checked. In addition, there is a demand and a need for cross borough and intercommunity transit that should be met. The existing transit lines run from outlying sections to the business sections of Brooklyn and lower Manhattan, like the ribs of a fan, with few facilities for cross traffic.

The construction of rapid transit lines, or even of surface lines, would take considerable time, even if money were available therefor. It would appear therefore that the present operation of buses, auxiliary to a comprehensive transit system, would furnish needed service promptly and at a minimum expenditure of capital.

The City has a large investment in the rapid transit lines built under Contract 4 and should be deeply interested in the financial results of operations thereunder. Consequently any increase in facilities that permits an improvement in the earnings under Contract 4 is in the direction of benefit to the City. Such improvement is possible by the immediate use of buses as feeder lines to terminal or intermediate stations from newly developed sections. Such operation, whether to transit stations or to surface lines, is also an added convenience to the public.

This Company is prepared to provide buses, modern, safe and commodious. A number of buses have already been acquired in order that the public may express its opinion as to the general type of bus that this Company is prepared to obtain and as an earnest that this Company will immediately equip the routes that may be agreed upon.

Consequently, application is hereby made to the Mayor and to the Board of Estimate and Apportionment of the City of New York for the granting of franchise or other proper legal permits for routes for the operation of buses. Without undertaking, at the present time, to specify all of the routes upon which bus operation is desirable, application is made for authority to place buses in operation on routes over the following or parallel streets:

1. *Kings Highway Route*—Kings Highway and Ocean Avenue through Kings Highway to

Buses

and through 22nd Avenue to Gravesend Bay and return.

2. *Brownsville Route*—Utica Avenue and Eastern Parkway, along Eastern Parkway to and along Pitkin Avenue, to and along Stone Avenue, to and along Sutter Avenue, to and along Barbey Street, to and along Glenmore Avenue, to and along Eldert's Lane to Liberty Avenue and return.

3. *Richmond Hill Route*—From Rockaway Boulevard, through Lefferts Avenue, to and through Jerome Avenue, to and through Sutphin Boulevard, to Hillside Avenue and return.

As to other similar routes, the Company will be glad to have the advice of the Board or of its representatives and it desires to reserve the privilege of submitting further suggestions.

If the City deems it desirable to grant authority for operation of such routes a separate corporation will be formed, under the Transportation Corporation Law, which will own and operate buses. Under the law, the Transit Commission will have jurisdiction of such corporation in respect to a certificate of necessity as to such matters as capitalization, accounts, character and safety of equipment and operation.

In order that the City and the public may be further adequately protected, the Company is willing to agree that the City be given access to the books and accounting of the bus company and absolute veto power on all capital expenditures as well as the veto power on the issuance of securities or stock by the bus company and the price at which such securities and stock shall be sold. We suggest that the rate of fare be one which will pay operating expenses, taxes, provide for necessary reserves and give a fair return on the capital actually invested. During an experimental period, to be agreed upon, the rate of fare upon the routes herein suggested shall be five cents. At the expiration of that period, the fare shall be adjusted by automatic provisions inserted in the franchise so as to accomplish the foregoing. Complete and adequate safeguards should be inserted in the franchise so that there is no profiteering and no extravagant rate of return and so that no financial jugglery could be possible. We are also willing to discuss with the City authorities the public advantage of a five cent fare for short hauls and a higher fare for longer hauls and the establishment of a scientific zoning system as well as the possibility of ultimately providing reduced fare transfers between bus, surface and rapid transit facilities. We again emphasize the limitation that there shall be not more than a fair return to the capital invested.

It is assumed that the City will recognize that operation by a separate corporation should produce sufficient revenue to pay the necessary and adequate operating expenses and reserves, and also a proper return on the amount of capital invested in the Company in order that operation may be permanent and that investors may be ready to aid in the further development of facilities for the public of this City.

City authorities have advocated the use of buses to aid in the relief of the public. It would appear, without discussing the financial conditions of the City or the principle of municipal ownership and operation, that the public would be well served by the operation of bus routes under the management of a large system already operating transit lines in which the City has a heavy investment

Buses

and upon which a return is essential if the City is to relieve taxes and have a debt margin with which to enlarge its transit system. Under such management, the public will be assured of proper maintenance of equipment and continuity of service.

This Company is prepared to undertake, under legal authority and proper restrictions, and with adequate and proper equipment and service, the routes herein stated and to co-operate with the City in the selection of additional routes.

Representatives of this Company are prepared at any time to confer with representatives of the City as to the details of proposed grants of authority, as herein requested, or as to routes, as well as a general plan of bus operation in the territory served in general, in Brooklyn and Queens, by B. M. T. Lines.

        Respectfully submitted,
        GERHARD M. DAHL, *Chairman*
        Brooklyn-Manhattan Transit Corporation.

On September 8, at the invitation of Chairman Delaney, President Menden and Vice President Whitney of the B. M. T. conferred with the Board of Transportation, which submitted the following two questions to them:

    1. Will the B. M. T. Company grant transfers from the bus lines which it proposes to establish to the rapid transit lines now under its control, and from those lines to the proposed bus lines, for a single five cent fare, the fares received by the bus lines for which transfers are given and used to be accounted for by the B. M. T. Company as revenue or earnings received by it under Contract 4?

2. Will the B. M. T. Company grant transfers from the bus lines which it proposes to establish to the trolley lines operated by it, and from those lines to the proposed bus lines without extra charge for such transfer?

In reply, on September 15, I wrote Chairman Delaney, that "We are extremely anxious to remove these questions and answers to them from controversy and, with your co-operation, to arrive at a result which will be beneficial to the public and fair to all concerned,

"We, therefore, submit the following propositions:

"A. We are willing to grant transfers (on the three routes specified in our letter of August 13, 1924) as proposed in your two questions for an experimental period of three months without asking any conditions other than that your board during the three months, shall take such steps as may be necessary to keep you fully informed as to the character of our service, our receipts and expenses, kept in accordance with the standards of accounting established by law or in pursuance thereof in respect of transportation companies in the State of New York.

"The result of this experimental period should be to furnish your board and ourselves with the data upon which we can base further negotiations.

"B. In the alternative, we are willing to grant transfers for a three months' experimental period on the above three routes, under acceptable franchises for such periods as the City and ourselves may agree upon, which shall require service at cost on our part and which shall contain appropriate provisions fully safeguarding the City and ourselves by clearly defining the various factors or items of service at cost.

"These factors, or items, are well known and long established. Necessarily a proper accounting standard would be required both in relation to the rapid transit lines and the surface lines.

"In order to have no misunderstanding, we wish to make it clear that we cannot accept franchises to transfer passengers free, if that course would result in our giving the service at an expense in excess of its cost.

"In any event, however, we are willing to make a three months' experiment at our own risk, as stated under paragraph A."

A few days later, in explaining this offer, I referred to the part transit plays in the development of a city and what a large factor the B. M. T. had been and could be in the further development of Brooklyn.

"The Company controls various trolley companies operating in Brooklyn and Queens. In addition, under Contract 4, the New York Rapid Transit Corporation (likewise controlled by this Company), operates Company lines and City-built lines, as one system on a five cent fare, with financial provisions whereby the Company applies the revenues, first, to operating expenses and reserves, second, to its agreed preferential and fixed charges on its investment, third, to fixed charges on the City's investment, and, fourth, equal division of remaining profits between the Company and the City.

"The City is, therefore, as a partner, interested in the financial outcome of operations. The revenues have never been sufficient to meet all of the Company's requirements under the contract. The consequence is that nothing has been paid to the City.

"The rapid development of Brooklyn under the stimulus of post-war activities and new transit lines,

Transit Truths

caused an increase in rapid transit travel on the lines operated by this Company from 226,515,512 in 1917 to 537,174,614 fare passengers in 1924, an increase of 137% in seven years. This increase in travel, coupled with favorable operating conditions, and a thorough reorganization in which the stockholders contributed $26,000,000.00, have improved materially the financial condition of the system. It is as important to the City as it is to the Company to do everything that will rapidly and still further improve that condition to the point where the City will be securing a return on its investment. There are two methods whereby the favorable rapid growth of Brooklyn may be encouraged.

"The first is the completion by the City of all construction work under Contract 4, namely, 14th Street-Eastern, Nassau Line, shops and yards and full length platforms. The importance of early completion of these in furnishing capacity for increased service to the public has already been indicated.

"The second is the establishment of bus routes in outlying and crosstown sections where transit facilities have not kept pace with development. These bus routes, therefore, should be supplemental to existing transit facilities in order that there should not be duplication of service when there are so many sections without any proper transit. The partnership of the City under Contract 4 should make it apparent that such bus facilities, pending extension of other transit facilities, should be furnished by this Company under supervision of the City. It is assumed that the City now desires to end present illegal bus operations and cause to be furnished to the public proper bus service under legal authorization, with lawful supervision of service, equipment, capitalization and accounts. It is further assumed that the public is willing to pay for additional and convenient service rendered to it."

After we had run the buses free over the three proposed routes in order to give the public "sample service" we received hundreds of requests to extend our bus service and many representatives of the civic organizations and public along the routes petitioned the Mayor and Board of Estimate to grant us franchises. Again the editorial opinion was unanimously in favor of our proposals.

Chapter IX.
Shops and Yards

CAR riders want service. As a rule their interest in transit is limited to their own needs. They want a train, a car or a bus "handy" when they want to travel. This is natural and normal.

If there were no politics mixed into transit, if it were a business, like the department store, or newspaper, grocery or restaurant, business men would provide complete transit service at a profit in time and convenience to the passenger and with only a reasonable financial return to the investors.

But strive as reasonable business men may, politics in New York City is ever present with the result that before the public can obtain service the people must be made acquainted with all the facts which make service possible.

One of the most important facts about service is that the operating company must have adequate shops for equipping and repairing its rolling stock and it must have adequate yards to conveniently store the cars during non-rush hours. This is so self-evident that it would not need to be emphasized were it not for the fact that the City of New York, after contracting to build shops and yards for the use of the rapid transit lines provided for under Contract No. 4, has refused for 11 years to live up to that agreement.

As there was no indication during the first fifteen months of the B. M. T. service that the City had any intention of keeping faith with the car riders and the Com-

Shops and Yards

pany, I addressed the following letter to Mayor Hylan calling his attention to "shops and yards" and their relation to the City's obligations:

>Brooklyn-Manhattan Transit Corporation
>85 Clinton Street
>Brooklyn, N. Y.
>September 11, 1924.

Hon. John F. Hylan,
Mayor, City of New York,
City Hall, New York City.

Dear Sir:—

On February 27, 1919, there was submitted to the Board of Estimate and Apportionment, "Report of the Committee on Finance and Budget of the Board of Estimate and Apportionment relative to the construction of those parts of the dual system of rapid transit railroads (Contracts 3 and 4) not yet placed under contract."

Acting upon this report, the Board passed a resolution which provided among other things, as follows:

>"RESOLVED, *That this Board does hereby declare and affirm its purpose to appropriate all necessary funds for the speedy completion of the Dual Subway System, when and as required.*"

That resolution was adopted over five years ago.

Under date of July 12, 1924, in a letter to Chairman Delaney of the Board of Transportation, I called attention to the urgent need of the City of New York living up to the obligations of its contract made in 1913 in three specific particulars:

1. Completion of the 14th Street-Eastern Line;
2. Construction of the Nassau Street Line;

3. Construction of shops and yards and full length platforms.

Later, attention was directed to the compelling reasons for the immediate construction of the Nassau Street Line. This can be completed in three years. It will allow 50% increase in rush hour service to the Fourth Avenue, Sea Beach, West End and Brighton Lines. The City of New York can relieve its long suffering public promptly and effectively by the construction of the Nassau Street Line. This will involve an expenditure of only about $12,000,000.00.

I now wish to emphasize that the obligation of the City to construct shops and yards is definitely fixed by the contract.

Since the date of the contract in 1913, no public official has denied the obligation of the City to supply shops and yards.

No one will deny that adequate shops and yards are necessary for the frequent and periodic inspection, repair and overhauling of cars, in order to keep them in safe and efficient operating condition.

On various occasions Your Honor has urged the importance both of a sufficient number of modern cars and of constant maintenance of equipment to a high degree of safety. With this we are in complete accord.

It is useless, however, to buy additional new cars if there is no place in which to equip or maintain them. If there is inadequate maintenance or inadequate equipment, it is because of the default on the part of the City for eleven years in its obligations to supply us with shops and yards.

Under our contract with the City, made in 1913, we included our existing shops and yards as a part of the

Shops and Yards

entire system to be operated on one fare, but the City was obligated to supply new shops and yards required as the system might develop after 1913. Since that time we have purchased 950 steel cars at a total cost of $20,000,000. For the maintenance of these cars the City has not spent one dollar in supplying shops and yards.

The Company is now completing the equipment of fifty new steel cars at an expense of $1,200,000.00. These were purchased since the reorganization took place in June, 1923. The work on these new cars is proceeding under the grave handicap of shops, inadequate even for routine work. It is plain that there is no use in buying new cars if there is no place in which to keep them in efficient operating condition.

So serious is the situation that the Company cannot consider the purchase of new cars for use on any part of the system, unless, by the time such cars are ready for delivery by the car builders the City shall have adequate shops available in which to equip such cars and, therefore, to maintain equipment.

The foregoing is but one illustration of the unfortunate situations which work to the detriment of the public and the public welfare.

It is realized that vital matters requiring immediate attention are frequently related to the dissatisfaction you have often expressed with existing subway contracts. This dissatisfaction does not, however, justify default by the City in performing important provisions of a contract which was entered into by due authority.

However, we do not like the contracts any more than you do, but, notwithstanding that fact, we have faithfully carried out all the provisions of the contract on our part. However, when two parties to a contract are dissatisfied

Transit Truths

with it, the sensible and business-like thing to do is to get together in an effort to readjust the contract. This we are perfectly willing to do. This we believe to be in the interest of the people of this community.

You have many times publicly stated that the debt limit of the City is an obstacle to subway construction. You have asked the Legislature to pass an amendment to the Constitution exempting $275,000,000.00 from the debt limit so that this amount would be available for subway construction. It is now apparent that such a constitutional amendment, even if adopted, cannot become effective until 1928. Therefore, the only form of relief which you have suggested appears to be so remote as to be practically useless.

Not only are we ready to discuss with you a readjustment of the terms of our contract, but we are willing to do so in an effort to work out a contract fair and in the interests of the public under which this Company itself will be able to provide the funds not only for the equipment but also for the construction of subways which are so urgently needed. We believe it is entirely possible to work out a plan whereby it will not be necessary for the City of New York to finance future subway construction.

We are in a position to make a firm commitment as to a substantial sum of money and we are willing to make a serious and earnest effort to provide sums in excess of the commitment which we are able to make—sums which will run into such large figures that nobody could make a firm commitment for them.

In brief, we are willing to co-operate in a definite and practical manner in filling the insistent need for more subways.

Meanwhile, I urge upon you not to lose sight of the

Shops and Yards

fact that service with equipment fully maintained is dependent upon adequate shops and yards. The B. M. T. system would be remiss in its duty to the public if it did not repeat and make clear the importance of the prompt construction of such shops and yards.

When you are prepared to inform the Company of the approximate date of the availability of such shops, the Company will then be in a position to place orders for new cars to be delivered by the time such shops are ready.

Yours truly,

GERHARD M. DAHL,
Chairman.

After a characteristic refusal by Mayor Hylan to consider seriously the proposals submitted in the foregoing letter, I made this public statement:

"It is quite evident that Mayor Hylan does not appreciate the seriousness of his flippant attitude toward the transit problems of this city. His sole weapon is abuse.

"By one stroke of his pen he publicly and officially assumes full responsibility for the terrible crowding now existing, for the delay in subway construction and the need for new shops and yards.

"It is evident that he refuses to admit the importance of our offer. We were willing and are still willing to finance all new subway construction, to build the Washington Heights Line; the Brooklyn Crosstown Line; the incomplete line to East New York; the Nassau link in lower Manhattan and new shops and yards.

"We were willing to do what the City has delayed doing for seven years and what the City cannot do in less than seven years more. In other words, the B. M. T. is ready and willing today to meet all the public needs for new rapid transit lines. It is ready to give the people the kind of service they need and desire.

"If Mayor Hylan does not want the people to have new subways and better service, the responsibility for further delays, further congestion and all future discomforts and inconveniences will be upon Mayor Hylan."

When Mayor Hylan declined to listen to our reasons for asking the City to keep its promises; when he brusquely brushed aside our offer to finance all the new lines needed by the public he aroused the daily newspaper editors to again demand action. This time, also, several of the editors of foreign language newspapers published in the Greater City expressed themselves emphatically in favor of ACTION.

"How much longer must we be crowded in the subways?" asked *Die Freiheit*. "Nero fiddles while Rome burns."

"One is unwittingly reminded of the above on entering a Brooklyn or New York subway. If you are not lucky enough to live at a terminal of the subway near the remote stations of the suburbs, you can be assured that you will not get a seat in the rush hours. Indeed, you will thank the lucky stars if you find a spot to stand upon. Often enough you will not need any spot to stand on; the jam will hold you suspended in the air, packed with others like sardines in a box. Seriously this is no exaggeration. Those who use the subways morning and night are well aware of the truth of the situation.

"A great deal has been said and written about this problem, but the only ones who seemingly have benefitted are those who have traveling facilities of their own. The strap hangers who suffer from the subways have found

Shops and Yards

very little relief from the meaningless talk and rhetorical statements made by politicians and newspapers. The cruelty of the situation is particularly aggravated because of the fact that the majority of the strap hangers in the rush hours are workingmen and women who have to toil the balance of the day. They are half exhausted when they reach their factories and shops. In what conditions can they be when they finally get home in that terrible crush after a day's hard work? Surely such a deplorable condition requires careful study and immediate action from the responsible officials of the city.

"What have they done, however, to find relief? What has our Mayor done? What has the Board of Estimate done about it? What does any of the numerous transit commissions do to relieve the situation?

"Nothing. They talk, investigate, ponder and talk some more. They throw the blame on the transit companies when other excuses fail. The transit company in turn blames the Board of Estimate, blames the Mayor. But of what use is this to the public? What benefit have they derived from these perpetual squabbles?

"Where once we could reach Manhattan from all sections of Brooklyn for a nickel we find that the Mayor's constant controversies with the B. M. T. has suspended some of the facilities such as the car service over the Williamsburgh Bridge. As a result thousands of people who travelled by car from Brooklyn to New York and who object to paying additional fare, now travel with the subway and elevated trains, and add to the already insufferable congestion.

"The Mayor's heart bleeds for the strap holders, we are told. He promised us seats in the subways. And what not! Nothing, however, has resulted either from his rosy promises or gloomy threats to the Company. The old subways are worse than ever and the new subways are more distant than before. The Brooklyn crosstown lines are still waiting to be built. The Nassau Street section has not been touched, Greenpoint Line is not yet completed, even the buses, which the Mayor promised, and which the B. M. T. is willing to run, have been blocked. How long will the New York public stand for it? How long will they be satisfied with empty political promises which mean so little? Have done with arguments! The solution lies in action, in digging subways, regardless whether the City or B. M. T. runs them. Better extensive and efficient transit system run by private capital than the present poor apology to be run by the city. The New York public needs immediate relief and cannot and will not wait for Utopian systems which the Mayor visualizes a quarter of a century from now.

"It is high time for action. It's up to the Mayor and the other City officials. They must come to an understanding with the present transit leaders to give the city prompt relief."

EDITORIAL OPINION

ABOUT NEW SUBWAYS: MAYOR HYLAN'S ATTITUDE

On September 15th the *Jewish Morning Journal* said:

"Mayor Hylan has again rejected with a quarrelsome gesture the proposition to do something about building new subways for New York. A proposition emanated from the B. M. T. to the effect that it was prepared to submit a plan whereby the B. M. T. alone would bear the cost of building several of the more im-

Shops and Yards

portant subway lines. The Mayor's angry "NO" even precludes the possibility of a conference.

"We don't know whether the plan of the B. M. T. is advantageous to the City or not. But one thing is certain, the Mayor's "NO" every time there is talk of relieving the unbearable subway conditions is becoming nauseating.

"The question is not whether the public is in love with the B. M. T. or the Interborough, or whether it is hostile. Let us admit that the transit corporations do not enjoy popularity with the public, and the subway question is not yet solved even by a hair's breadth. The question in which the public is intensely interested is: Will there be new subways and how soon?

"Every time when it is necessary to answer this simple question, we hear from Mayor Hylan, instead of plain words, only quarrelsome language and attacks on this or that company. Does Mayor Hylan really think that you can constantly feed the New York public with vulgar attacks, instead of building subways?

"Eleven years ago the city entered into several contracts to build new subways. Now, after the lapse of eleven years, only a small fraction of a new subway line is opened up, the 14th Street-Eastern Line, and this line is suddenly terminated in an out of the way section of Brooklyn, without connection with any of the important subway lines, so that it is almost useless. The other lines the city has failed to build in accordance with the terms of its contracts, because Mayor Hylan has plans for a network of municipally operated subways. But this is only music for the future, because the City has neither the funds for that purpose, nor could these subways be completed within less than several decades, even if the City had the funds.

"Meanwhile the crowding and discomfort in the existing subways is growing worse and worse, without any sign of relief.

"Mayor Hylan should look about to see where in the world he is 'at.' Soon a new Mayoralty election will be on, and if he maintains his present attitude, his record will be a very sorry one indeed. The public demands new subways and not new quarrels."

The *Amerikai Magyar Nepszava,* another foreign language paper, published the following editorial, entitled: "How the B. M. T. Would Like to Better Subway Service."

"New York's leading officials have said many times that they are not satisfied with the contract which was made five years ago with the B. M. T., because this contract does not provide for the changed conditions today. The interesting point in this case is that the B. M. T. subway is also dissatisfied with this contract.

"Gerhard M. Dahl, chairman of the B. M. T., in a letter to Mayor Hylan points out the failure to live up to this contract and offers to change the terms of the contract to meet the changed conditions.

"Chairman Dahl, in a previous letter, stated that there is an immediate need of the following:

1. The completion of the 14th Street Line.
2. The building the Nassau Street Line, and
3. The building of new yards, repair shops and enlarging of the platforms at the subway stations.

Shops and Yards

"In the past few years the subway traffic has so largely increased that the completion of the 14th Street and Nassau Street Line is a necessity. The lack of repair shops, yards and platforms hinders efficiency in work. Since 1913 the city has not built new yards and repair shops, but the city insists that the B. M. T. put new steel cars in operation. The B. M. T., in fact has bought 950 new steel cars for $20,000,000, according to the contract. In the past year they built 50 new steel cars, which cost $1,200,000. To the building of new cars the city has contributed nothing.

"Chairman Dahl also points out that the building of the new cars cannot improve the service because the platforms are not long enough to accommodate longer trains in front of them.

"In spite of all these arguments which Mr. Dahl advances, the City is still claiming that the service given by the B. M. T. is not sufficient. Therefore, Mr. Dahl asks the Mayor to change the contract so that the subway company may be able to give better service to the public. Mr. Dahl is sure that there is a way to remedy these conditions.

"Mr. Dahl says that the B. M. T. is in a position to raise the funds which are necessary for the completion of these lines and also to build new yards, repair shops, platforms and cars."

The New York *Times,* in an editorial entitled, "Rapid Transit Finance," said:

"The spokesman for that portion of the dual subway contracts which most concerns Mayor Hylan's home borough 'represents the interests,' of course. But that is no excuse for refusing to discuss how the city can build and finance more rapid transit facilities. The interests are willing either to proceed according to the city's contract or to amend the contract as may be mutually agreed. For seven years the city has declined to do either.

"The Brooklyn company has provided more steel cars than it is possible to send through the subways, yet the city authorities continue to blame it for using wooden cars. The city has refused to build, as it contracted to do, the tracks for the steel cars to run on, or yards in which to equip and repair them. The loops are necessary for switching trains, and the contract for operation would never have been signed without the provision of that operating necessity. The city's partner has provided $20,000,000 worth of additional cars, but the city has not spent one dollar for the loops or yards indispensable for getting the cars through the subways.

"Before Mayor Hylan took office he approved the dual subway plans as regards the Brooklyn portions. Years after the contracts were signed the city officially approved the particular portions here discussed, though they are unfinished after eleven years of obstruction. The result is that the city is more underbuilt in rapid transit than in housing, and both riders and renters are sufferers for the sake of the Mayor's politics. If the interests could be made to suffer alone, there might be votes in it. But the electorate is discovering that the passengers and the carriers have concerns in common. Distribution is the remedy for congestion. Increase of rents as an alternative is worse than an increase of fares.

"The Mayor is in his last ditch on rapid transit finance. The funds he talks of finding are gold at the end of the rainbow. People in this city are tortured by a policy which compels the majority to try to live within a ribbon of territory a mile wide along the subways. That cannot

Shops and Yards

go on indefinitely. Mayor Hylan must do something soon for rapid transit or lose that popularity which is to him dearer than life."

"Eleven Years and Nothing Done" was the editorial caption in The *World*.

"People who are fated to use the subways instead of automobiles provided at the taxpayers' expense may not all approve Mayor Hylan's haste in rejecting the proffer of co-operation made by Chairman Dahl for the Brooklyn-Manhattan system.

"In his letter to the Mayor Mr. Dahl had urged the completion of the 14th Street Line, the construction of the Nassau Street link and the provision of shops and yards and full-length platforms which the city had agreed to make in its bargain of 1913. It is useless, as Mr. Dahl says, to buy new cars 'if there is no place in which to equip or maintain them'; at a cost of only $12,000,000 the Nassau Street Line 'will allow 50-per-cent increase in rush-hour service to the Fourth Avenue, Sea Beach, West End and Brighton Lines.'

"Mr. Dahl and his associates 'believe it is entirely possible to work out a plan whereby it will not be necessary for the City of New York to finance further subway construction.' This plan the Mayor refuses even to discuss, though he has had to abandon hope of relief in less than four years by the dubious route of constitutional amendment.

"So if the Mayor's view prevails, nothing can be done for subway relief for a long time. The city will not keep its promises. Eleven years under contract and nothing done to fulfill it will hardly seem to subway-users a satisfactory record."

Chapter X.
Common Sense Transit

ON August 26, 1924, at the request of The New York *Evening Post,* I wrote the following article:

"Uncle Joe" Cannon once said that reformers "damn everything over a foot high or a year old."

Here in New York City there are a lot of politicians who follow this policy in discussing transit questions but as Abe Martin would say, this may be the right way to catch voters but "it don't git nowhere."

Transit conditions will never be improved, new subways will never be built and the public will never obtain what it needs and demands if this attitude continues.

Ever since the organization of the Brooklyn-Manhattan Transit Corporation in June, 1923, this Company has endeavored to fulfill a three-fold public duty, first, to provide the best service possible with its equipment despite the political handicaps, second, to improve its facilities and increase its rolling stock, and third, to make public *facts,* without which an understanding of transit problems is impossible.

This is nothing more than a common sense policy.

After one year of activity we have discovered that it takes common sense a long time to make headway against the political hecklers who continue to "damn everything over a foot high or a year old." They have no regard for the facts or for the truth. Because of this political policy of damnation the people of the city are no better off today than they were a year ago except for the constructive work of public-spirited citizens. As far as the City officially is concerned, it has delayed transit relief seven years and Chairman Delaney has just admitted that it will be from five to seven years more before the public may expect adequate relief. If the policy of the City continues the public will be no better off seven years from now than it is today.

Thus we come to the real human problem in this City which is: How can the people be helped to tell the difference between facts and political bunk? Public opinion is the most powerful factor in transit today. It will be a bigger factor tomorrow. Public opinion can compel construction. Public opinion can solve every problem of transit in less than one year by using facts and common sense.

Transit is entirely a human problem. Human beings manage and operate the lines to transport human beings. Investors and taxpayers are human beings. Together their combined forces give public opinion its authority and power.

It seems to me there is every reason why their common interests should lead eventually to common action for the common good.

The interests of the B. M. T. and the public are identical.

1. *Financially.*

In the first place, this Company is owned, controlled and directed by public interests. Politicians speak of "Traction Interests." Suppose we analyze this phrase and apply it to the Brooklyn-Manhattan Transit Corporation.

The largest individual owner of the Corporation

is the United States Government. Through the War Finance Corporation "Uncle Sam" has $21,000,000 invested in the B. M. T.

In addition to "Uncle Sam" 16,000 private investors, many of them daily passengers, are stockholders.

Eight out of every ten B. M. T. employees are stockholders, having recently oversubscribed an offering of 15,000 shares of preferred stock.

Furthermore, every taxpayer and rentpayer has a financial interest in the Corporation because the City of New York has $150,000,000 invested in our rapid transit lines.

Do not these facts prove that the controlling financial interests are public interests?

2. *Public Policy.*

When the Brooklyn-Manhattan Transit Corporation was organized, leading public-spirited citizens who had no financial interest in the Company were invited to become public directors. Six men, from the three boroughs, Brooklyn, Queens and Manhattan, served by the B. M. T., accepted the invitation. Three directors were appointed by the New York State Transit Commission. In addition, a director was selected by the U. S. Government, acting through the War Finance Corporation. These men have served the *public* on our board for more than a year and they are continuing this service, convinced that the Company is actuated by a real desire to fulfill both the letter and spirit of its obligations to the people of the city.

Every time any problem has come before the directors it has been decided solely on the basis of public interest. This applies to safety, service, improvements and extensions quite as much as to the rights of investors and taxpayers who have an honest financial interest in the soundness and security of transit as a public business.

3. *Improvements.*

The B. M. T. today is operating 950 steel cars. To appreciate the significance of this statement it should be pointed out that in 1913 when the Dual Contracts were signed it was estimated that only 600 steel cars would be required *after* the construction work was fully completed. But to date the City has not completed this work. It has not finished the 14th Street-Eastern Line. It has not even started the Nassau-Broad Streets Extension. It has not built the shops and yards. Thus the Company today is operating 350 more steel cars than it was estimated would be necessary. Furthermore, these 950 steel cars now tax the capacity of the shops and yards. Only recently the Company spent $150,000 on its shops because, in the public interest, it could not wait for the City to live up to its contract and build the shops and yards agreed upon in 1913.

Finally, the Company is ready to put more steel cars in service as soon as the City builds the yards and shops to accommodate them. This is an obligation and a duty of the City.

During the first fiscal year the B. M. T. appropriated $4,000,000 for improvements and new equipment—and this policy of building up the physical assets of the Company will be continued.

Furthermore, the Company has urged new construction as a public policy. While the City is obligated by contract to complete the 14th Street-Eastern and Nassau Lines the Company has taken the position that the public welfare demands more transit lines. I have said repeatedly in public statements that while the B. M. T. expects the City to live up to its contract, the Company favors additional lines whether operated by this Company or not.

Recently the Company purchased 10 new, modern buses and petitioned the Board of Estimate for franchises to operate them over three specific routes in Brooklyn.

Every one of these activities is in the public interest.

And still, despite these efforts, despite the public ownership of B. M. T. securities, despite the attempts of the Company to meet the best interests of the public, both the Company and its officials have been damned by politicians.

After all, public sentiment is going to determine what shall be done. Public opinion will guide not only those in office but to a large extent the press and all other moulders of opinion. There are two classes of leaders. In one class are those who always follow what they think is public sentiment regardless of whether it is right or wrong. This class always appeals to public prejudice and never to reason or conscience. In the other class are those who believe in moulding and creating public sentiment so that it is right and never fears public sentiment when it is wrong. In that class are those who appeal to conscience and reason and sound common sense.

Now the general attitude of the public towards transit companies in Greater New York is critical and hostile. The spontaneous reaction of the public to anything emanating from a transit company is one of skepticism and the natural and immediate reaction to any criticism, or even abuse of the transit company, is one of enthusiastic applause. The good intentions, the good faith, the honorable conduct of those in charge of transit companies are all suspected. What is the reason for this?

There are two reasons. First, there have been many abuses in the past by public service corporations. The public has suffered from unscrupulous financial manipulation, from unconscionable corruption on the part of those in charge of utilities—corrupt public officials. There has always been a public be damned attitude—an attitude completely disregarding the welfare and the desires and the needs of the public. These abuses on the part of the companies led naturally and logically to attacks by public officials, newspapers and the public generally, but the pendulum always swings too far. The pendulum swung too far in the direction of special privileges to the public utilities and abuses on their part such as described above and now the pendulum seems to me to be swinging too far the other way. Dishonesty, corruption, disregard of public needs and rights and comforts all led to just criticism and now there is frequently unjust criticism. To begin with, there are some who never know nor care what the facts are, and they assume that the road to popularity is to criticise a transit company. And so they criticise. On the other hand, there are those who in perfect good faith and with the best of intentions, criticise transit companies, but without sufficient knowledge of the facts. In fact, an explanation to them and an understanding by them of the facts frequently converts unjust criticism into sympathetic understanding.

And so the real problem of the transit companies in Greater New York today is to have the public understand the facts. This, of course, is on the assumption that the transit companies themselves today are not guilty

Transit Truths

of the abuses of the past; that they are anxious to serve the public; to obtain the public good-will and to deserve public good-will; that they are not guilty of either dishonest or financial jugglery or manipulations to the detriment of their properties. And this I maintain is the situation today, but the public does not know it. It doesn't make any difference how good a case you have if the public does not know it.

We have to expect that, but all the damns in their vocabulary will not interfere with our program of doing the best we can to provide service and to present facts to the public because we know from long experience in business that big, intricate problems like transit cannot and will not be solved by politicians. They will have to stand on the side lines shouting their abuse while public-spirited citizens get things done.

But, no matter how public-spirited business men may be, they cannot move any faster than public opinion. Fortunately for the people of this city the newspapers have an interest in *facts,* the clergy is interested in facts, the women are keenly alive to the importance of facts and as fast as facts can be put to work we may expect progress.

EDITORIAL OPINION

On the same day the foregoing article was printed The New York *Evening Post* said editorially:

"If there are any residents of this city who are inclined to listen seriously when Mayor Hylan launches a rhetorical attack upon the transit 'interests' they will do well to read what Mr. Gerhard M. Dahl says on the point in his article in today's issue of this newspaper.

"The biggest 'interest' in the Brooklyn-Manhattan Transit Corporation, which is the particular object of the Mayor's hostility just now, is Uncle Sam, who has $21,000,000 invested. With him are 16,000 others, including eight in every ten of the company's employees.

"In the transit lines as a whole these investors are thrown into the shade by Father Knickerbocker, who has no less than $150,000,000 invested. The biggest transit 'interest' in this municipality is the City of New York.

"Whatever the city Administration does in order to injure the existing transit companies is, therefore, a blow at the financial soundness of the Federal Government and the treasury of New York City. Refusal to make connections with existing lines is refusal to allow the city to share in any financial benefit that might result from such connections. Nothing would please the present Administration better apparently than to see the transit companies go on indefinitely with no profit whatever. The people of this city should realize that this condition would mean no return on the money the city has invested. The bonds by means of which it has raised this money will burden the taxpayers until they are paid. There is no honest way of dodging this fact.

"So long as the city gets no profit from the transit lines the money it has put into those lines counts against the debt limit. Once the lines pay, the $150,000,000 represents a self-supporting enterprise and comes out of the amount to be charged against the city in ascertaining its borrowing capacity. Thus the city would gain doubly by a sensible transit policy.

"The biggest 'interests' in the transit situation, however, are not financial. They are the 6,000,000 human beings whom the Hylan do-nothing program is inconveniencing and endangering. These are the 'interests' which the Brooklyn Chamber of Commerce has in mind when it puts to Mayor Hylan the two questions: 'What are you going to do? When are you going to do it?'

"The people of this city have a right to an answer to these questions. The only satisfactory answer that can be made is the adoption of plans and the letting of contracts for new subways. Promises have ceased to be interesting. What is required is action."

Chapter XI.
Municipal Ownership

FOR 10 years prior to December 1, 1923, the B. M. T. and the Brooklyn City Railroad Company operated local trolley service and through trolley service over Williamsburg bridge. The City of New York, however, desiring to further its program of municipal operation interfered with this regular service by inaugurating its own local service across the bridge, thus forcing the companies to discontinue their service.

The companies at that time stated publicly that they could not maintain through service at a further financial loss when the City deprived them of the profitable short haul.

Under private operation the public received three tickets for five cents for the local bridge service, or one ride for two cents.

On October 1, 1924, without advance notice to the public, the City increased the fare 20 per cent.

At that time public opinion again found expression in editorials in the press.

"When municipal operation of the Williamsburg Bridge trolleys was urged in 1920, a report to the Aldermen predicted that the experiment would 'prepare those in charge the better to grapple with the problem of municipal operation which confronts the city in its larger aspects,'" said the *Evening World*.

"The present 'grapple' results in a 20 per cent. increase in fares on the ground that 'those in charge' are unable to prevent the collectors from appropriating the odd third of a cent from the 2-cent cash fares. The B. M. T. somehow managed to prevent this petty pilfering, or at least failed to use it as a pretext for higher fares. So instead of 5 cents for three rides under the B. M. T. the charge will now be 6 cents for three rides.

"But this is less than half the story. The B. M. T. claimed that it made profit enough from local service to warrant free service for through passengers. The city collects from both classes of patrons. It has roughly twice as many pay passengers as the B. M. T., but is unable to show a profit.

"Local service patrons must pay 20 per cent. more for municipal service. Through service patrons must pay 5 cents plus 2 cents, or 40 per cent. more, and must endure the inconvenience and delay of changing cars in any sort of weather.

"Under the circumstances does the experiment in municipal operation show improved and cheaper service, or have 'those in charge' been thrown for a loss in the first 'grapple?' "

"The result is that notwithstanding the increased income which the City now enjoys," observed the Jewish Daily *Forward,* "and despite the tens of thousands of dollars which the private companies earned, the City is losing money, on account of which it increased the fare, and the City will gouge the public to the extent of seventy thousand dollars a year more than the private companies.

"This is an unheard-of scandal. This is the sort of mismanagement which savors of the good old days of wholesale graft."

"So This Is Municipal Operation," said The New York *Evening Post.*

Municipal Ownership

"When the city established a straight 2 cent fare on the Williamsburg Bridge shuttle in place of the former arrangement of three tickets for a nickel it excused the increase on the ground that conductors were 'knocking down' fares. They would collect 6 cents from three passengers who paid in cash instead of in tickets, drop three tickets into the box and pocket the odd cent. Upon being informed of this excuse Transit Commissioner Harkness exclaimed: 'So this is municipal operation!'

"The five words characterize the entire history of the Williamsburg Bridge shuttle under the operation of the city. Indeed, they are an appropriate comment upon the part the city has been playing in the whole matter of transit relief.

"Mayor Hylan chose the Williamsburg Bridge shuttle for the deliberate purpose of giving a demonstration of the advantages of municipal over private operation. The first 'advantage' resulting from municipal operation was the imposition of an additional fare. Under private management, through passengers had been carried from Brooklyn to Manhattan for 5 cents. There was a shuttle service for persons who merely crossed the bridge. Three shuttle tickets were sold for a nickel. By taking over the shuttle service the city forced the companies off the bridge. As a consequence, through passengers had to change cars and, incidentally, pay for the privilege at the rate of three tickets for 5 cents.

"Persons who merely crossed the bridge did not experience the 'advantages' of municipal operation so promptly, but their turn was coming. By a midnight order the fare on the shuttle cars was suddenly increased 20 per cent.

"One point in this increase deserves special notice.

It could not have been made in this abrupt manner by a private company. Such a company would have had to submit a request for the increase to the Transit Commission, just as a privately operated public utility of any kind in this State cannot increase its rates without first appealing to a Public Service Commission. There would have had to be a hearing. The company would have had to justify its proposal for an increased fare by showing that its line was economically and efficiently managed. The city was under no such necessity. All it had to do —and all it did—was to post a midnight order.

"The story of the city's experiment with the Williamsburg Bridge service cannot be better told than in the crisp phrasing of Commissioner Harkness: 'The sum total of the city's mistaken activities is to break up a through service, compel thousands of passengers to transfer from one set of cars to another and make them pay 7 cents instead of 5.'"

"Mr. Hylan Submits a Sample," said the New York *Herald Tribune.*

"For seven years Mayor Hylan has insisted that if he were intrusted with the right to build and operate municipal transit lines fares would be reduced, congestion would be relieved and the transit problem would be automatically solved. Recently he has said that if the Legislature would exempt from the debt limit $275,000,000 for subway construction purposes, and give its spending into his hands, he would guarantee relief within sixty days.

"Many of Mr. Hylan's friends, knowing his views about municipal ownership, have wondered why he has consistently refused to accept any of the municipal operation plans which have been suggested and why he has done nothing whatever toward subway construction and operation, even after the power he had been demanding was conferred upon him. Recently the reason has become apparent.

"In a year of municipal operation of the Williamsburg Bridge shuttle line a profit of $60,000 a year earned under private ownership totally disappeared, and a loss of $40,000 was shown. The Commissioner of Plant and Structures, who has been in office only a few months, declares that this loss is due wholly to unpreventable pilfering of fares by conductors on the line. The only remedy he has to suggest is that the fares be increased, so that there will be something left for the city after the conductors have taken what they have become accustomed to taking.

"Now, if Mr. Hylan, with the power of appointment of conductors on a line less than a mile in length, cannot keep them from stealing, how would he be able to keep the thousands of employees picked by him to run a great city transit system from absorbing a far greater sum? And if Mr. Hylan loses a hundred thousand dollars a year on a single shuttle line, how many millions a year would he lose were he to run the entire transit business of the city?

"Neither the Interborough nor the Brooklyn-Manhattan Transit managers complain of losses due to theft. Nor will the people of the city readily believe that transit employees are generally dishonest. But if Mr. Hylan, who is and will be under obligations to his political organization, is unable to pick honest men to pull his bell punches on this inconsequential little road, is he likely to be any more fortunate in his judgment of human nature when he exercises unlimited powers over transit?

"Mr. Hylan in the operation of the Williamsburg Bridge shuttle submitted a sample of municipal operation. It is not a sample that is likely to sell his municipal operations to the taxpayers."

"The incident is more than a mere example of efficiency in dealing with alleged graft of one cent in six," observed The New York *Times,* "The loss to the passengers far exceeds that to the City. Each passenger who might have ridden across the bridge for nothing under private operation was compelled to continue his ride from the local bridge car at either end of the bridge. This loss of transfer privilege extends to all city-managed routes, present or proposed. The City cannot give transfers off its own routes. If transfers are to be given, they can be made most useful only on a universal system of interchange."

Chapter XII.
Public Officials

IN fifteen years I have had the good fortune to successively experience all three viewpoints of the public utility problem: the viewpoint of the officer of the municipality, that of a public service commissioner and that of counsel for utility companies," W. A. Magee, Mayor of Pittsburgh, said, speaking on October 7, 1924, at the 43rd annual convention of the American Electric Railway Association, at Atlantic City.

Referring to the problems of the industry and the "disaster" which the World War inflicted upon public utilities, Mayor Magee declared:

"The other point requiring effort is the education of the public to a full recognition of the fact that municipal growth as well as the public comfort and convenience is dependent upon financially sound utilities.

"A public servant is useless to the public if the public will not give him the resources necessary to the execution of their will. The utility company is the public servant as much as the officer who receives his office by direct vote of the people. Preventing the charge of sufficient rates by a public service company is analogous in the life of the city to forbidding an adequate tax rate. A too-low tax rate prevents standards of municipal service demanded by the public. A too-low street car fare prevents a company from rendering service according to the standards demanded by the patrons which is only another name for the same public. A refusal of the city electorate to use the city credit through bond loans for the improvement of needed streets, sewers, playgrounds and parks is no less short-sighted than opposition to street railway fares that will permit the company to gain the credit necessary to float loans for the extensions and improvements of the company's property and service which the public expect. The rate of a utility company is identical with the city tax rate. The utility officer can no more serve the patrons, that is, the public, with bare hands than can the municipal officer. There is no distinction between the two cases except that in the first case the public understand the consequences because the operation is a more direct one. In the case of the utility company it is only more roundabout.

"The municipal officer knowing the analogy between his position and that of the utility officer and also because he occupies a point of vantage from which he knows or should know the conditions and circumstances of the utility enterprises within his jurisdiction owes a moral duty to his constituents to lead them in the formation of their opinion and in the expression of their decision with relation to the utility companies. Sometimes his duty will tell him that he should stand in the face of public opinion, sometimes his duty will require him to enter into contest with the utility company. He should have the courage to do either and he should feel that in either event the initiative rests upon him rather than upon the patrons of the company who are not conversant with these highly complex questions in the manner that he is. There has been a broad, deep chasm separating the two parties to an issue that one time seemed insoluble. Five years ago the future of the railroader and the utility companies of the land had a dark outlook indeed. Now it is all changed, a more enlightened public opinion, and the public service commissions trained by a study of the problem have, with the aid of the courts, done wonders. The local public officer, I regret to say, has not played the role that was open to him, but some have and the number is constantly growing, who appreciate their responsibility, and who are rising to the occasion."

Index

A

Subject	Pages
Abuse	5, 91, 105
Accounting System	61
Action	18, 92
Advertisements	10, 51
American Electric Railway Association	115
American, New York	51
Amerikai Magyar Nepszava	96
"Are Public Servants Worthy of Their Hire"	51, 52
Ashland Place Connection	11, 33, 38, 39, 41, 43, 44
Astoria, Map	66
Atlantic City	115

B

B. M. T.
    Directors 11, 21, 22
    Employees 73
    Maps 43, 62, 66
    Mileage 10
    Reorganization 9, 15
    Stock Ownership 73
Baltimore 34, 48
Barton, Bruce 16
Belford, Monsignor John L. 46
Better Metropolitan Transit 15, 24, 25, 38, 44
Board of Estimate 60, 77, 93
    Dual Subway Resolution 87
Board of Transportation 10, 57, 59
Boody, Charles A. 22
Boston 34, 35, 48
Brighton Beach Line 12, 24, 42, 67
    Map 62
Broadway Subway 42
    Map 62
Bronx 47

Index

Subject	Pages
Brooklyn (Borough)	10, 20, 21, 24, 35, 41, 42, 53, 65
Map	62, 66
Brooklyn Chamber of Commerce	23
Brooklyn City Railroad	109
Brooklyn Crosstown Line	33, 44, 53, 60, 91
Brooklyn Times	10
Brownsville Bus Route	79
B. R. T.	19, 23, 30, 35
Brush, Matthew C.	23
Buffalo	34, 48
Building Construction	12
Build More Transit Lines	57
Bulletin, New York	71
Buses	11, 76, 82
Letter to Mayor	77
Bus Fares	79
Bus Routes	77, 80

C

Canal St.	36, 38, 39, 41, 45, 65, 67
Map	58, 62
Canarsie Line	66
Cannon, "Uncle Joe"	100
Capital	30
Buses	80
Car Riders	13, 26, 27, 47, 59
Centre Street Loop	42, 67
Chambers Street	42, 43, 67
Map	58, 62
Chase National Bank	18
Chicago	34, 35, 48, 51
Cincinnati	49, 51
Citizen, The Brooklyn	45
City of New York	25, 30, 33, 35, 36, 39, 40, 45, 47
City's Investment	29, 47, 61
Civic Council of Brooklyn	26
Cleveland	15, 16, 17, 48, 49
Commissioner	
Dahl, Gerhard M.	16
Delaney, John H.	44, 52
Common Sense	9, 100
Comptroller	33
Coney Island	62, 66

[120]

Index

Subject	Pages
Congestion	13, 41, 45, 65, 68, 98
Constitutional Amendment	90
Contract No. 4	11, 30, 36, 39, 40, 43, 47, 59, 60, 61, 63, 64, 67, 69, 70, 78, 86
Buses	81
Revision	89
Co-operation	25
Corona Line, Map	66
Cost of Operation:	
Cleveland	49
Detroit	49
New York	51, 60, 68
Seattle	50
Cost of Service:	
Cleveland	17
New York	31, 32
Culver Line	42
Map	62

D

Dahl, Gerhard M.	13, 23
Biography of	15
Dallas, Texas	49, 51
Davis, James Sherlock	22
Debate	52
Deficits	32
DeKalb Ave.	39, 41, 42, 67
Maps	62, 66, 72, 73
Tracks, Number of	43
Trains Per Hour	68
"Delaney and Dig" or "Delaney and Delay"	See Adv. Following Page 72
Delaney, John H.	44, 52, 55, 57, 59, 71
Bus Conference	81, 82
Promise of 1920	See Adv. Following Page 72
Refusal to Build Nassau	See Adv. Following Page 72
Delay:	
11 Years' Delay	36
Denver	51
Detroit	34, 48, 49, 51
Directors	21, 38, 39, 102
Names of	22
Dividends	75
Dual Subway Contracts	19, 45

Index

E

Subject	Pages
Eagle, Brooklyn Daily	44, 55, 71
Earnings	37
East New York	40, 43, 45, 91
Editorials	15, 44, 45, 55, 71, 106
Electric Bond and Share Co.	17
"Eleven Years and Nothing Done"	99
Employees	73, 75, 102
English, William H.	22

Equipment:
    Shops and Yards Needed 69
Evening World 109

F

Fares 11, 19, 27, 28, 31, 32, 34, 35, 37, 46, 48, 49, 51, 60
    Bus Fares 81
    Compared to Cost 47
    Table of Fares in U. S. 48, 51
    Williamsburg Bridge 109
Finance New Subways 90
Forward, Jewish Daily 110
14th Street-Eastern Line 11, 31, 33, 35, 36, 38, 44, 47, 57, 65
Fourth Ave. Line 38
Franklin, George S. 22
Freiheit, Die, Editorial 92
French Lick 52
Fulton St. Line 38

H

Hylan, Mayor John F. 10, 12, 57
    Approved Dual Subway Contracts 98
    Breach of Contract 71, 96
    Bus Letter 77
    Challenge to Debate 52
    11 Years' Delay 95
    Freiheit Editorial 92
    "Mayor's Heart Bleeds" 93
    Policy .... See Adv. Following Page 72
    Promises 56
    Quarrelsome Gesture 94
    Refusal to Heed Offer to Finance Subways 91
    "Rhetorical Attack" 106
    Salary Increase 51
    Utopian System 94

Index

Subject	Pages
Vulgar Attacks	95
Williamsburg Bridge	111, 112, 114
Harkness, Commissioner LeRoy T.	111, 112
Herald Tribune, New York	112

I

Illegal Bus Service	84
Improvements	11, 103
Indianapolis	48
Interest	31
Investors	13, 20, 26, 27, 28, 29, 30, 32, 47
Investors' Experience, Table of	37
I. R. T.	19, 29, 46, 113

J

Jamaica Board of Trade	46
Jamaica Line, Map	66
Jewish Daily Forward	110
Jewish Morning Journal	94
Johns, William H.	22

K

Kansas City	51
Kings Highway Bus Route	78

L

Lawrence St. Station	12
Legal Obligations	68
Legislature	57, 112
Constitutional Amendment	90, 112
Look Ahead	24, 46
Losses	20, 29, 61

M

Magee, Mayor	115
Malbone St.	24
Manhattan	10, 21, 24, 35, 43
Manhattan Bridge	42, 43, 67, 68
Maps	58, 62, 66
Marling, Alfred E.	22

Index

Subject	Pages
Martin, Abe	100
Materials	20, 21
Mayer, Judge Julius M.	23
Mayor of New York	(See Hylan, John F.)
McAneny, Chairman George	57
Menden, William S.	18, 22, 24, 39
Bus Conference	81
Letter to Employees	73
Montague Street Tunnel	43
Municipal	
Buses	80
Operation	48, 49, 109, 110
Service	110, 112
Myrtle Ave. Line	40

N

Nassau Street Line	11, 31, 33, 35, 36, 38, 40, 42, 44, 103
Cost	88
Map of	58, 72, 73
"Nero Fiddles," Editorial	92
New Orleans	15, 18
New Subways:	
Offer to Finance	90, 92
New York Stock Exchange	20
N. Y. & Queens Co. Railroad	51
N. Y. Rapid Transit Corp.	59, 70

P

Partners	19
Passengers	20, 84
Philadelphia	34, 48, 51
Pittsburgh	34, 35, 48, 51
Mayor Magee	115
Platforms; Lengthen	69
Post, James H.	22
Post, The New York Evening	45, 100, 106, 110
Preferentials	30
Preferred Stock	75
Press	9
Private Operation	48, 51, 109
Providence	48, 51
Public Directors	21, 102

Index

Subject	Pages
Public Officials	115, 117
Public Servants	51, 115

Q

Queens	10, 20, 21, 24, 51, 68
Buses	81
Map	62
Queensboro Chamber of Commerce	26

R

Rapid Transit Act	60
Rapid Transit Finance	97
Receiver (B. R. T.)	44
Receivership	19
Referendum	9, 12, 15
Rentpayer	102
Richmond Hill Bus Route	79
Richmond, Virginia	48
Rush Hour Service	69, 88

S

Safety	11, 102
Sargent, Charles S., Jr.	23
Scandal	110
Sea Beach Line	41
Map	62
Seattle	48, 50
Securities	21
Shaw, Robert Alfred	22, 38, 39
Shops and Yards	36, 65, 68, 69, 84, 103
Letter to Delaney	59
Letter to Mayor	86
Shuttle	111
Sinking Fund	31
Smith, Governor Alfred E.	See Adv. Following Page 72
Somers, Arthur S.	22, 23, 24, 39
Standard Union	15, 44
Steel Cars	11, 12, 21, 97, 103
Cost	89
St. Louis	34
Stockholders	20, 35, 84

Index

Subject	Pages
Stock Ownership	73
Strap Hangers	93
Strauss, Frederick	23
Subways, Cost of	36

T

Tacoma	50, 51
Taxes	49
Re Buses	79, 80
Taxpayers	9, 26, 27, 29, 30, 31, 32, 35, 36, 47, 59
Taxpayers' Investments, Table of	37
Times, Brooklyn Daily	45, 71
Times, The New York	71, 97, 114
Toledo	51
Traction Interests	101, 107
Trains:	
Per Hour	67
Full Length	69
Transfers	11, 40
Transit Commission	10, 38, 51, 57, 60, 65, 70, 102
Buses	79
Transit Facilities	12
Tribune, New York Herald	45
Trolley	11
Truth	5
Tunnel, Need of New	44

U

Uncle Sam	107
Unification	63, 64
Union Square	58
United States Government	73
Investment in B. M. T.	102
Universal Service	9, 57
Utica Ave. Line	12
Bus Route	79
Utility Company	115

W

Wages	20, 21
War	34, 60, 115
War Finance Corporation	102
Washington, D. C.	48

Index

Subject	Pages
Washington Heights	33, 44, 60, 91
West End Line	41
Map	62
Whitehall Street Tunnel	43
Whitney, Travis H.	18, 22, 39, 81
Wiggin, Albert H.	23
Williamsburg Bridge	58, 67
Fare Increase	109, 113
Map	62
Williamsburg Power Plant	11
Wisconsin	16
Wooden Cars	12
World, New York	99
Wyckoff Ave.	40

Z

Zoning System for Buses	80

Date Due

HE
4491
.H58
D13

Dahl, C.M., 1876-
Transit truths
... 1924.

Printed in Dunstable, United Kingdom